Making Meetings Work:

*A Guide for Leaders
and Group Members*

Leland P. Bradford,
Ph.D., L.H.D.

Pfeiffer
& COMPANY

Amsterdam • Johannesburg • London
San Diego • Sydney • Toronto

Copyright © 1976 by University Associates, Inc.

ISBN: 0-88390-122-6

Library of Congress Catalog Card Number: 76-16886

Printed in the United States of America

The materials that appear in this book may be reproduced for educational or training activities. Special permission for such not required. However, the following statement must appear on all reproductions:

This permission statement is limited to reproduction of materials for educational or training events. *Systematic or large-scale reproduction or distribution—or inclusion of items in publications for sale—may be done only with prior written permission.*

This book is printed on acid-free, recycled stock that meets or exceeds the minimum GPO and EPA specifications for recycled paper.

CONTENTS

FOREWORD

This is an amazingly useful book, distilled from great wisdom and years of experience in working with groups and then looking back on their meetings and reflecting on what was helpful or unhelpful. Lee Bradford was more responsible than any other single individual in the development of the movement known as group dynamics, which grew out of the creative writings and work of the great German psychologist, Kurt Lewin. Dr. Bradford was one of a small group that founded the National Training Laboratory in Group Development (now the NTL Institute of Applied Behavioral Science) in 1947. Since that time, thousands of people have learned from him and his co-workers how to work more effectively and constructively as members and leaders of groups.

In view of the fact that most of us spend a large part of our working hours in groups of one kind or another—family, work groups, classes, and meetings—it is clear that an understanding of our own and others' behavior, feelings, and satisfactions can be extremely useful. Drawing on extensive research and his own long practice, Dr. Bradford has distilled in this small volume a treasury of helpful ideas for those who find themselves in positions of leadership, or who want to be helpful members of the groups in which they participate. Happily, the author is very skillful in bringing together practical suggestions of "what to do" with clear explanations of why certain kinds of behavior produce the results they do.

In a time like the present, when there is a growing resentment of authoritarian behavior, and a great desire for participation in decision making, this book can help all of us learn that it *is* possible to involve everyone, and that there are ways to ensure freedom, fairness, and productivity in any group. In this bicentennial era, it is refreshing to realize once again that democracy really can be effective and satisfying.

CYNTHIA C. WEDEL
National Chairman of Volunteers
The American National Red Cross

INTRODUCTION

Thousands of individuals become group leaders with little experience and a minimum of training. Most of them have acquired these leadership roles by election, volunteering, seniority, desire to serve, or job responsibility.

Many have done well in the leadership position, but few have done as well as they could, given the various subtle attitudes, skills, and understandings required of good leadership, and the ever-changing behavior in the groups they lead. Leaders face many challenges:

- How to turn apathy and indifference into involvement and concern
- How to create a group from a collection of individuals
- How to manage difficult members—the long-winded talker, the constant disrupter, the member with an ulterior purpose, the member who gets the meeting off-the-track, the joker, and many others
- How to use conflict constructively
- How to prompt silent members to participate
- How to maintain control of the meeting
- How to arrive at a decision
- How to ensure implementation of decisions

Knowledge of the complexities of group interaction and appreciation of the dynamics of leadership behavior can do much to improve productivity in group meetings and ease the strain on leaders.

In communities all over America, countless meetings are held each year in schools, churches, clubs, hospitals, health organizations, volunteer groups, and business offices. Organizations—industrial, educational, governmental, scientific, service, health—conduct daily or weekly meetings of staff members for various purposes. State, regional, and national organizations hold annual conferences. A multitude of training organizations conduct sessions of various lengths. The costs in time and money reach astronomical figures, while the results are usually small. Why are some meetings productive and others a waste of time? Some plausible answers to that question might result from analyzing a number of meetings.

A Company Meeting

■ The president of a company holds his weekly Monday morning meeting with his vice presidents. After he makes a few comments urging redoubled efforts, he asks the several vice presidents to report on their operations. All reports are generally favorable. However, the vice president for engineering says offhandedly that some of his staff feel the research people have no idea how difficult it is to retool for new products. Somewhat heatedly, the vice president for production adds that no one has any idea how hard it is to retrain workers for new tasks. It might be cheaper, he says, to fire old workers and hire new ones. At that, the face of the personnel director reddens, but he says nothing. The vice president for marketing complains that one of the problems his people face is selling new products. Finally the president interrupts in a soothing voice, saying that the company must keep ahead of the field and he is certain they will work it all out.

After the meeting, the president reflects that while there was some acrimony, it probably was good because the competition stirred up energy that could lead to increased effort.

A trained observer watching this meeting would have noted that the initial comments made by the president had several effects. Rather than building a team of which he was a part, the president separated himself from the group by requiring each person to report to him. His comments were considered judgmental and punishing by the vice presidents. By pitting each vice president against the other, he helped create a sense of individual separateness rather than team membership.

Reporting was the central purpose of the meeting. If the group had faced a company-wide problem, they all could have become involved in solving it. Then the vice president for research would not have become the obvious scapegoat, something that enabled the others to play one-upmanship and feel more secure.

By the bland closing of the meeting, the president avoided responsibility for the infighting and indicated that teamwork was not really considered a serious goal. By ignoring the slightly camouflaged conflict, he established a pattern for such conflict and closed the door on resolving the issues.

The Volunteer Organization

■ The semiannual meeting of a volunteer organization is in session. The agenda is ritualistically structured. First, the lengthy minutes of the previous meetings are tediously read and approved. Next, the president calls upon the chairpersons of several committees. They read their reports, again at length. These are approved. The president reports on her tenure in office, describing her accomplishments but failing to mention some unsolved problems that are bothering some of the members. Candidates for offices are named by the nominating committee. They are duly voted into office for the coming year. Mentioning the lateness of the hour, the president asks if there is any other business. After a short moment of silence, a motion is made for adjournment. It is quickly seconded, voted upon, and the meeting ends.

As they leave the meeting, several members express regret that certain irritating problems were not brought up. They quickly excuse themselves from responsibility by reflecting that the president did not appear to want the problems brought up, and perhaps some group was already working on them.

A trained observer would conclude that this organization is having difficulty in involving its members. Officers seem to take positions from a sense of duty, but have difficulty in mobilizing committees into action. Members criticize the actions of the organization freely to each other, but no one analyzes the periodic meetings.

If time had been taken, perhaps first by a subcommittee and then by the total group, ideas for improving organization meetings could have emerged. The very process would have helped to spark interest and involvement.

The Social Club

■ The Social Club meets monthly for luncheon and the chairperson always has a difficult time planning the meeting. To make the meeting inspirational, a speaker must be located who will say the right thing in the right way. Each month the chairperson hopes the luncheon meal will be better than the last one.

A trained observer might see that no one in the organization has found a purpose for meeting that really excites and involves the members. That is why each succeeding leader tries to locate some outside person to save each meeting. The only purpose of the monthly luncheon seems to be to provide a reason for the members to see and be seen.

Most likely, any initial effort to get the members to suggest new ideas would buck tradition unsuccessfully and be met with apathy. However, if each incoming chairwoman had mailed a simple questionnaire to all members at the beginning of the fall, ideas would have been gradually generated. People generally support what they create or decide upon, and thus members would show more interest.

The Committee

■ One small committee, a part of a larger community organization, has been meeting at regular intervals for the past few years. While the original purpose of the group had been a noble one, this purpose has been lost in the difficulties the committee is experiencing within itself. Two persons are at swords' points with each other. Every meeting is disrupted by the sometimes subtle, sometimes open, conflict between the two. The committee chairman talks to each person privately, but each, while promising to try to avoid future conflict, blames the other for the trouble.

Another member of the group is a compulsive talker. He always has quite a bit to say about any subject brought up in the committee. As he seldom listens to others, his comments are usually irrelevant, lengthy, and boring. The committee leader talks to him privately, but there is no change in the situation. The leader tries to think of what else to do, short of pounding on the table and telling the member to keep quiet. Once he tries to resign the leadership but is persuaded to continue. Privately he thinks the group should disband and he wonders why people continue to attend meetings.

A trained observer would conclude that the chairman's error lay in absolving the total committee of any responsibility for the conduct of its members and for its own ineffectiveness and lack of productivity. By not encouraging the group to handle its working problems, he was, without being aware of it, preventing the committee from becoming a close-knit, concerned, and productive group. His actions allowed the group to remain a collection of individuals and allowed some members to act out their own problems to the detriment of the group.

The committee members, accustomed to the leader assuming responsibility for group behavior (irritated though some members might be at the actions of others), colluded with the leader by sitting back and enduring the futility of each meeting.

The idea that a leader should be controlling rather than sharing the responsibility for group behavior serves to maintain a low level of group effectiveness and perpetuates the belief that groups are hydra-headed monsters that accomplish little work.

The National Conference

■ A committee is meeting to plan the annual conference of a national organization. The leader of the committee wants this year's conference to be superior to all previous conferences.

As the first problem, the committee tackles selection of an overall theme for the conference. Committee members want the theme to be timely, catchy, newsworthy, and broad enough to include almost any program they might desire. A member suggests a theme that, after being worked over, satisfies the committee.

The next order of business is selection of the best possible speaker to give the opening inspirational talk. Another equally prominent speaker must be procured for the banquet to be held on the eve of the final conference day as an incentive for people to stay over. A long list of candidates is winnowed down to practical possibilities, and the chairman is authorized to go down the list until he has secured two speakers.

Meeting forms for the conference are considered. It is decided that one major meeting will be held each day, along with numerous smaller meetings to cover what the committee assumes to be special interests of various subgroups within the total membership.

One major meeting will be a panel discussion between some leading members of the association. After a long discussion, the president of the association is asked to serve as moderator of the panel, in part because he is present and the committee members are making a nice gesture. Some committee members have private reservations concerning the president's skills at effective orchestration of the panel speeches, but the decision is made and the president accepts.

A list of topics for the afternoon discussion groups is drawn up. The committee decides to have a number of discussion groups but to limit each one to an hour so that people can attend several such groups during the conference. Persons known by committee members are recommended as discussion leaders, and some time is spent in pairing these suggested names with topics.

Numerous other minor decisions are made and committee members are assigned to various tasks. A final meeting of the committee is scheduled close to the conference dates as a check on progress.

A trained observer would perceive an implicit assumption behind the planning of this conference: Those attending should be inspired, instructed, entertained, pleased, but not involved deeply in problems they face back home. Participants should dutifully attend the major meetings, but they are expected to spend much of their time drinking with friends and sightseeing, using the conference as an opportunity to travel and as a break from the routine of daily work.

Also implicit in the planning was the leader's desire to be successful and to be rewarded for providing well-known inspirational speakers.

The discussion groups were included as a concession to a modern trend in conferences, but the committee was careful to keep the discussion time short so that no group would have time to disrupt the plans of the committee. In choosing discussion leaders, the major criterion was ability to keep discussion under control.

These brief illustrations give some indication of the range and diversity of group meetings that require competent leadership. They also raise many questions, both about leadership and group behavior:

- What is the function of leadership? To command? To control? To reward and punish members and the group? Or to assist members to work effectively together and to build a group capable of regulating itself?

- What should be the basic philosophy and purpose of leadership? To dominate and police, or to serve and assist? What skills are required to support such a philosophy of leadership?
- What are the individual behaviors that disrupt or help a group? What are the cues to such behaviors? The motives? Who is responsible for helping members to be less disruptive and more helpful? The leader? Other members? Both? Is agreement with all points, or silence, necessarily helpful?
- What are the many intricacies of group behavior? What are their causes? How are they recognized? By whom? How are they dealt with? By whom? What is the leader's responsibility? To handle problems? To teach members?
- How can groups be helped to grow? How is teamwork fostered or discouraged? What is the leader's responsibility? The members' responsibility? How are members encouraged to take responsibility for group behavior and productivity? How is responsibility carried out?
- In what ways can a member function helpfully? When? How can he learn these skills?
- How can a group learn to regulate and improve its behavior and effectiveness? What should and can the leader do to assist in this process?
- What are the stages of group growth? What are the characteristics of an ineffective and immature group? Of an effective, growing, and mature group? What should and can the leader do to assist in the process of group growth?
- What traditions keep groups and meetings of all sizes and purposes from being more productive?

Leadership can become a successful and rewarding experience with (1) an adequate understanding and acceptance of the functions of leadership; (2) the diagnostic skills to understand ever-changing group behavior (its effect upon individual behavior and the effect of individual behavior on the group); and (3) skills in assisting members and the group to become self-regulatory and self-developing.

CHAPTER

TRADITIONAL LEADERSHIP AND A NEW APPROACH

What is leadership? How does a leader lead? Is leadership the task of one designated person, or is it a series of functions performed by the entire group? The beginning leader will find many different and confusing answers to these questions, because leadership is viewed in many different ways. This initial chapter will contrast the traditional beliefs about "ideal" leadership with the findings that have emerged from the contemporary study of group functions and leadership behavior.

The Traditional View

In the traditional view, the leader is chosen from a selected few who have the initiative and power to direct, drive, instruct, and control those who follow. The leader's task is to get the job done as efficiently and quickly as possible. Six "shoulds," or expectations, follow from this definition of the leader's task.

1. *The focus should be fundamentally on the task.* The task to be done and the goal to be achieved are all important. Although members (and the leader) undoubtedly have feelings and reactions about the group task, or may have hidden motives for being in the group, those issues have no place in the meeting. When topics not directly related to the main issue are introduced, arguments develop, or boring speeches begin to waste time, the leader should politely, but firmly and decisively, stop all disruptive acts.

2. *Group members may advise, but leaders should make decisions.* The leader calls meetings to hear the opinions of the members. If possible, he tries to get agreement, but he reserves the right to make decisions privately. He will endeavor to get a quick vote before too

many points of view create confusion. Group members are probably unable to make good collective decisions; if decision making were shared, it would make lines of authority and responsibility unclear, and confusion rampant.

3. *Interaction should be ignored as much as possible.* Although members interact with each other while the group is in session, their interactions and personal feelings toward each other are secondary to the task. Factors such as group morale and cohesiveness will tend to take care of themselves. The members' attention should be directed to the agenda and their ideas orchestrated by the leader.

4. *The leader should stay in control.* As their number increases, members are likely to become more diversive, divisive, irresponsible, and engage in aimless discussions and polemic conflict. Because the meeting often can be led astray by aggressive or attractive members, the leader must always be on his toes to observe and counteract proposals at variance with the best decision he strives for. Strong and forceful leaders are required.

5. *The leader should maintain a power position.* Leaders are leaders because their competence and prestige have been recognized. Most group members seem to welcome a strong leader who can exert control and provide safety and security for weaker members. The leader needs to be watchful for threats to his power and should fight, if necessary, to maintain his authority.

6. *Feelings should be dampened.* The task of the meeting requires logical thinking, not emotional outbursts. Members should be discouraged from expressing feelings rather than facts. If conflicts surface, the leader should remind the group members that maturity demands emotional control and that the group should strive to be objective. On occasion, the meeting can be adjourned until members calm down.

These traditional leadership practices produce results. Decisions are made—and often unmade at the next meeting. Members carefully address remarks to the leader and order is maintained. But often at a cost. Sometimes valuable contributions are not made because the discussion is so tightly controlled. Members may feel apathetic and uninvolved. Conflicts between members smoulder under the surface, forcing ineffective compromises. Frequently, members complain among themselves that the meeting was railroaded and their time was wasted.

The traditional task-oriented approach to leadership focuses most of the power, authority, and responsibility on the leader. If resources of members are denied or ignored, then energizing forces are driven underground, and the members never learn to accept responsibility.

Decisions come rather easily in task-oriented leadership. The critical problem arises when the decision is to be implemented. Because members have had no real part in making the decision, they often have little enthusiasm for carrying it out.

Group-Centered Leadership

There is another, quite different approach to leadership. Over the past forty years, a considerable amount of research and experimentation with leadership functions has yielded an abundance of useful information for the leader and the group with which he works. This approach—the group-centered approach—prescribes certain kinds of behavior for all group members, including the leader. While fully recognizing the importance of the group's task, this approach also takes into account the complexities of group behavior. Member interaction and the needs, purposes, and emotional reactions of individuals have a profound effect on the task solution and, therefore, need to be understood and appropriately dealt with.

LEADERSHIP IS A SHARED FUNCTION

Leadership is not something that just the designated leader does. Leadership happens when any intervention by the leader or a group member moves the group forward toward three goals: the accomplishment of the task, the resolution of internal group problems, and the ability of the members to work together effectively as a group. The designated leader shares the leadership role with all the members.

By recognizing that leadership is a group function to which all members can contribute, the leader helps to develop a sense of teamwork and group cohesion. The sharing of leadership (and the recognition, satisfaction, and feeling of power that accompany it) ensures that all the resources of the group will be used productively.

The effective leader knows that no one person can possibly be sensitive to all the task, group-maintenance, group-building, and individual problems existing at any moment in the group. Such sensitivity requires the combined watchfulness of a number of persons—all the group members. Some members may be more aware of task functions that are needed, such as information seeking and critical appraisal. Others may be more aware of group-maintenance needs, such as helping the quiet member to participate. Still others may be more adept at helping particular members to understand how, perhaps unconsciously, they are disrupting the group, while others aid in developing teamwork.

LEADERSHIP INVOLVES ACTIVE LISTENING

Knowing the complexity of group behavior and the interaction between feelings and the task, an effective leader listens actively to the task discussion to determine when specific functions are required—such as summarizing, clarifying, focusing, and preventing too rapid closure of discussion—and encourages group members also to listen for needed functions and fill them when required. At the same time, the leader endeavors to recognize and diagnose verbal and nonverbal cues that indicate the intrusion of hidden agendas and disruptive individual behavior that could be harmful to the group's productivity. If these issues are sufficiently disturbing, the leader brings these cues to the attention of the group, checks to see if others have made the same observation, and suggests that the group explore and deal with the disturbing situation. By this kind of intervention, the leader helps members become aware of both task and group problems and of the need to deal with such problems appropriately.

LEADERSHIP INVOLVES BUILDING AND MAINTENANCE

A major task for the designated leader is to work toward the building of a mature, productive group. As a group continuously is built and maintained, its members increasingly accept responsibility for recognizing and solving internal problems and for helping various group members improve their membership ability.

The designated leader can work toward building and maintaining the group in many ways. He can suggest that interpersonal problems be brought out in the open and resolved. When he observes withdrawal on the part of some members, or difficulty in arriving at a decision, or overparticipation by a few, he can suggest taking the time to diagnose the difficulty and to work out solutions until the group can perform at more productive levels.

Members of most groups are aware of difficulties and disturbing events. Members need a sanction to discuss internal group problems in a constructive manner in the group rather than outside of it. Methods of handling internal problems are not very difficult to learn. Helping members to diagnose destructive or disturbing behavior and to intervene constructively enables them to build more productive groups and to conduct more effective meetings. All members can enhance their awareness of group maintenance, group building, and interpersonal problems, while they work on task problems.

LEADERSHIP IS SERVICE

The leader who is concerned with involving all members in building and maintaining a productive group views leadership as service and assistance to the group. Such service includes helping the group to develop a climate of trust, enabling members to express freely their feelings, reactions, or evidences of trouble within the group without fear of reprisal. It includes helping members to see how they can help the group accomplish its task. It helps the group recognize, surface, and deal with internal problems that disrupt the meeting. A conflict between members is not only a problem for those concerned but also for the whole group. The leader can encourage the group to accept conflict as a group problem and can assist the members to bring it to the surface of discussion and work through it so that they can then return to their task. No matter how much members might prefer to ignore the conflict, such a difficulty inhibits group movement. In short, a leader may serve as facilitator, consultant, adviser, teacher, observer, or participant.

Because he believes in the responsibility and ability of group members to reach decisions, maintain and develop the group, and help each other learn how to be more effective participants, the leader actively encourages the involvement of the members.

LEADERSHIP REQUIRES ATTENTION TO COVERT EVENTS

Feelings and emotions; individual purposes and hidden agendas; interpersonal likings and dislikings; competitions and conflicts; reactions to the agenda issue and the consequences of its solution; feelings about the leader, either dependent or antagonistic; moods of the group; pressures from outside groups; or past experiences with the same group—all are legitimate facts that have impact on the group's work. These covert issues are as important to make overt as the listed agenda. In fact, items on the listed agenda frequently cannot be resolved until the emotional climate within the group surfaces and is worked through. Effective leaders know this.

The competent leader believes that conflict, brought to the surface and worked through constructively, provides an experience of success for the group—reducing the fear of conflict and strengthening the group for future crises.

The leader faces conflict calmly as a natural and common event, but he encourages the group and the particular members involved to look at the root of the conflict and find ways to reconcile it.

LEADERSHIP INVOLVES A GROUP—NOT A COLLECTION OF INDIVIDUALS

The effective leader sees the group as a group—not merely as a collection of individuals. Such a leader perceives the group as a whole and realizes the extent to which morale or feelings of satisfaction can change within the group. A group may change from working effectively to seeking ways of avoiding task responsibility. The effective leader understands that all feelings, emotions, and reactions of members, and of the group as a whole, have a profound effect on the trend of the discussion and the adequacy of the decision or solution reached.

Groups of any size can, by proper meeting methods, arrive at solutions or decisions about issues with which they are concerned. The size of the group has little to do with participation. If appropriate methods are utilized, meetings and conferences of up to a thousand persons can assure active participation of all in the issues to be discussed. The myth of ineffective meetings and irresponsible group behavior can be dispelled.

The contrast between traditional leadership and group-centered leadership is summarized as follows:

TRADITIONAL LEADERSHIP	GROUP – CENTERED LEADERSHIP
1. The leader directs, controls, polices the members, and leads them to the proper decision. Basically it is his group, and the leader's authority and responsibility are acknowledged by members.	1. The group, or meeting, is *owned* by the members, including the leader. All members, with the leader's assistance, contribute to its effectiveness.
2. The leader focuses his attention on the task to be accomplished. He brings the group back from any diverse wandering. He performs all the functions needed to arrive at the proper decision.	2. The group is responsible, with occasional and appropriate help from the leader, for reaching a decision that includes the participation of all and is the product of all. The leader is a servant and helper to the group.

3. The leader sets limits and uses rules of order to keep the discussion within strict limits set by the agenda. He controls the time spent on each item lest the group wander fruitlessly.

3. Members of the group should be encouraged and helped to take responsibility for its task productivity, its methods of working, its assignment of tasks, its plans for the use of the time available.

4. The leader believes that emotions are disruptive to objective, logical thinking, and should be discouraged or suppressed. He assumes it is his task to make clear to all members the disruptive effect of emotions.

4. Feelings, emotions, conflict are recognized by the members and the leader as legitimate facts and situations demanding as serious attention as the task agenda.

5. The leader believes that he should handle a member's disruptive behavior by talking to him away from the group; it is his task to do so.

5. The leader believes that any problem in the group must be faced and solved within the group and by the group. As trust develops among members, it is much easier for an individual to discover ways in which his behavior is bothering the group.

6. Because the need to arrive at a task decision is all important in the eyes of the leader, needs of individual members are considered less important.

6. With help and encouragement from the leader, the members come to realize that the needs, feelings, and purposes of all members should be met so that an awareness of being a group forms. Then the group can continue to grow.

CHAPTER

SOME REASONS FOR
INEFFECTIVE MEETINGS

Many meetings waste a lot of time. Even the best meetings are not as productive as they could be. In this chapter, some common reasons why meetings fail to accomplish their goals are described.

Research in Leadership Functions and Group Process Is Relatively Recent

Fish, the adage says, are the last creatures to discover water. Even though human beings spend most of their lives in groups, the systematic study of group process and its impact on group productivity is relatively recent. New skills of leadership and new methods of conducting meetings have been discovered and perfected, but there has not been time for this information to reach all the people who need it.

Risk Taking Is Difficult

Leaders are not born to leadership; they become leaders through learning experiences. It takes time to learn sensitivity to group process, awareness of group phenomena, and the skills required to intervene appropriately. Many leaders, schooled in traditional beliefs about leadership, hesitate to try newer methods lest they appear weak and inadequate in front of group members. Taking the risk of sharing decision making or of dealing openly with the group conflict and emotional behavior requires courage and commitment. A fear of experimenting can result in ineffective meetings.

People Attend Meetings for Reasons Beyond the Task at Hand

Even inadequate meetings and conferences serve the needs of people to feel powerful and included. The designated leader can feel proud and powerful in his devotion to the task, and these feelings may compensate for all the frustration he experiences. As he uses his position and power to bring the meeting to the end he desires, the leader is viewed with respect and admiration, attitudes which strengthen his self-image. Power, authority and status are a heady mixture, even though stress—"keeping the meeting on the beam" and controlling aggressive and recalcitrant members—is the price that is paid.

For members there are a number of values that may outweigh frustration, anonymity, and lack of power. Being a member provides the individual with a feeling of belonging without paying the price of responsibility. Belonging—whether to a group, committee, or association—means that some others do not belong. Self-identity develops from many factors and one is the recognition that one belongs. If one is a member of a powerful inner group—a vice president of a company or organization—a considerable amount of power and prestige results; the weekly fight to maintain position in the pecking order is not too high a price to pay for the power gained. The struggle to gain or retain prominence over others results in the need to "size up" other members, to decide, often stereotypically, who are friends and who are opponents, and accordingly, to devise secret strategies.

Meetings may also provide the latest information and gossip. In meetings, a self-serving remark judiciously camouflaged can appear as a contribution to the decision. And meetings can interrupt the routine of dull work.

Conference going, whether or not one attends any of the meetings, can contain many advantages for the individual. The home newspaper may report his attendance. Neighbors eye him respectfully. Travel to another city leaves memories to be recalled. The individual can gain status by commenting about his experiences in casual conversation with those who did not attend. Old friendships can be renewed at the conference, and strategic persons can be added to one's list of acquaintances. Appearance at the conference may ultimately lead to some prestigious association position.

The individual's personal needs to feel powerful, acknowledged, and included are legitimate, and they can better be met openly through involvement and shared leadership functions rather than by such remote connections to meetings and conferences.

Democracy Takes Time

Shared leadership, group decision making, and consensus—the hallmarks of the democratic group—take time, trust, and openness.

Shared leadership raises the threat that a subgroup or coalition of members will "railroad" a decision. Therefore, decision making by a group is easily inhibited by a leader who rewards or punishes members for their contributions. Even consensus—allowing all group members to influence the decision—can lull group members into believing that decision making is their primary task and that implementing the decision is someone else's job. Effective decision making should always include planning for implementation.

Often, participants collude, avoiding responsibility by requiring the presentation of more facts and more data, with the full knowledge that sufficient facts to satisfy everyone will never be produced. Relegating the decision or its implementation to a subcommittee is another common tactic.

Leaders face a grave dilemma—how to live with ineffective meetings and still get difficult decisions made. The answer for most leaders is obvious. Thinking through the problem ahead of time, a leader often comes to a few alternative ways of reaching his goal. If his power is great, the leader's slanted presentation of the issue gives cues to group members. Summarizing at a strategic moment can stop debate. Comments such as "I don't see where that idea fits in" or "That's an idea we might take up later" are usually guaranteed to squelch ideas not wanted by the leader. Consequently, a façade of open, democratic group decision is maintained by tight controls exerted by the leader.

Democracy takes time. The democratic group fails when efficiency acquires more importance at the expense of respectful consideration of individual needs to express thoughts and feelings, work through differences, and be involved in a final decision.

"We've Always Done It This Way"

Ritual and tradition keep many meetings as they presently are. Throughout the country, in organizations, churches, schools, and community groups, meetings are held at a customary time and place, whether or not there is a need for the meeting.

Ritual and tradition are used commonly in other ways. Cumbersome procedural methods, such as Robert's Rules of Order or similar rules (occasionally necessary for legal purposes), produce a dull and long-drawn-out meeting.

Breaking ritual and tradition is difficult. Few group members want to "stick their necks out" for fear of rejection or possible misunderstanding of motives. Some leaders hesitate to suggest new methods lest they be viewed as "one-upping" the previous leader or as confusing the members.

The old adage that "There isn't any reason for it, it's just our practice" becomes a deterrent to improvement and change. Individuals may grumble privately at the waste of their time at meetings, and they may fail to go to sessions at conferences that they have traveled hundreds of miles to attend. So strong is habit, however, that if the meetings or conferences were not held, suspicions might arise that some plot was afoot. Meetings, groups, and conferences have always been this way, and members have little expectation of change.

Many group meetings exist to prevent decisions that might disrupt the status quo. In the name of preserving tradition and ritual, the leader and the group members seem to conspire or combine forces to prevent change.

Environment Has Impact

The physical environment has an impact on the productivity of the meeting. The room arrangement helps to determine the extent of free and open participation, and the shape of the table reflects communication patterns.

Some examples of room arrangements will illustrate the extent to which these arrangements encourage leadership power and control and inhibit inter-member communication.

The conference room in many companies and organizations is oblong in shape and often rather narrow, and so is the conference table. The leader sits at the head of the table, his position symbolizing both his power and authority as well as giving him a clear view of all members and an opportunity to control or respond to any member statement. Sometimes by his side sits a secretary, notebook open and pencil poised, ready to take down whatever the leader would like to record. This alerts members to be extremely careful in what they say.

In some meetings, specific seating arrangements indicate a pecking order or hierarchical structure in the organization. Those higher in power and position sit nearer to the leader on each side of the table. Those with less influence sit farther away, in descending order, from the head of the table. Obviously these members are aware that their verbal contributions will be less well heard than those emanating from members farther up the table. More vocal energy and ego strength will be required for them to participate actively.

A variation of the long, narrow table is a hollow square or a deep well formed by four tables, with the distance between each table making participation and discussion difficult.

Another meeting arrangement, with consequences for involvement and participation of those attending, is the common situation in which rows of chairs face the front of the room where the leader or speaker has a table or rostrum, placing distance—both physical and psychological—between the audience and himself.

A curious phenomenon generally occurs before the meeting. As members straggle in, they tend to fill the seats from the middle to the back of the room, putting distance between themselves and the leader or speaker. Late-comers are thereby forced to take the front seats. This disengagement or uninvolvement seems to signal that the audience is there to listen, not to participate verbally unless called upon. Discussion, if any, flows generally only between the leader and one or two of the participants. Only a master speaker can bridge the gap between the stage and the audience.

Although these physical arrangements remain as common practice, round or square tables are increasingly used in meetings, or no tables are used at all, enabling everyone, including the leader, to communicate directly. But in many situations, especially diplomatic conferences, the shape of the table is a major concern and with good reason: physical arrangement can enhance or inhibit productivity.

These considerations account for the ineffectiveness of many meetings. They indicate the impact of the traditional expectation that the responsibility for the meeting's success rests squarely on the leader. As leaders accept the responsibility to plan, maneuver, and control whatever happens, they assume the impossible task of performing all functions necessary for an effective meeting, while at the same time they are trying to keep members involved.

These considerations describe the strong forces resistant to change. Many leaders and members have no hope that meetings can be improved, nor do they have the skills to bring about the improvement they desire. The general low opinion of the quality of group interaction is reinforced by long experience with inadequate meetings.

Yet many leaders would like to increase the involvement of group members and improve the quality of decisions made by groups. The next few chapters look at various aspects of group behavior and meeting functions.

CHAPTER

CLUES TO
GROUP DYSFUNCTION

Every meeting involves three simultaneous operations: task activity, maintenance, and team building. The *task activity* refers to work on the stated agenda: issues to be discussed, problems to be resolved, decisions to be reached. *Maintenance* requires keeping the group in good working order by attending to the needs and purposes of the members—how they feel toward each other and toward the task. *Team building* refers to any activities that strengthen the group's capacity to face future issues successfully.

In an effective, fully functioning meeting, all three operations will receive some attention. If the group needs to attend to a member's personal feelings or problems, it does so, and then returns to the task. If an opportunity for developing problem-solving skills among members occurs, the group diverts from the task to do some team building.

Many groups, however, are unable to consider all three operations; some groups even have trouble dealing with one. In some instances, because of internal events, the group cannot do its task, much less attend to maintenance or team building. These internal events are familiar to anyone who attends meetings; they include reactions against the task, conflict, faulty communication, apathy, fear of making decisions, and ineffective interaction among members and leaders.

Reaction to the Agenda

A negative reaction results when members cannot solve a problem, when they are frustrated by insufficient information, or when the meaning and consequences of the task are not clear to them. Sometimes, members are dismayed or angered because a certain agenda item is to be discussed. At other times, members may regard the task as a waste of time because someone with more power than the group will ultimately make the "real" decision.

Conflict Within the Group

Conflict, which may occur between individuals or subgroups, can reflect the unspoken purpose of some members to block a majority decision. It may be a way of punishing or blocking the leader. Permitted and sustained by the members, it can serve as an excuse for avoiding the main agenda item. Conflict frequently occurs when two or more members compete for influence in the group. Pressures from outside groups, which some members feel that they represent, also may create conflict.

Lack of Communication Skills

If the leader and members are unable to express their views well, or are poor listeners, communication may become garbled. The members may lack assertiveness and allow aggressive, controlling members to take charge and dominate the meeting. Shy members may not be able to express authentic support for good ideas or confront others in constructive disagreement.

Apathy

Unhappy or unproductive experiences with the group promote lack of interest and a sense of hopelessness in members. They may have no opportunity to participate or to influence group decisions. They may feel dominated by the leader, lack interest in the group's purpose, or be thoroughly bored by windy speeches and endless discussion.

Fear of Decision Making

Decisions often threaten a meeting and its members. Decisions involve taking responsibility and risking error. They may disrupt cherished programs or create problems with outside forces or other groups. Some members may try to shape or prevent decision making to accommodate their loyalties to other groups. Decisions mean more work for someone, and there is no assurance that even good decisions will be implemented.

CLUES TO DYSFUNCTION

Major problems may exist in any group meeting, but they can be faced before the group deteriorates if clues to potential dysfunction are recognized early. When the leader and members recognize these clues and openly focus attention on them, they are learning to diagnose group problems, and they are taking steps toward their resolution. If the clues are ignored, work on the agenda issues may be futile.

Avoidance of the Task

Frequently, when a group dodges the main issue and talks instead about extraneous or picayune points, something is keeping the members from real work. They may:

- fear the size and consequences of the main problem;
- feel inadequate to deal with the issue;
- lack the desire to work hard;
- feel uninvolved;
- feel hostility or fear toward the leader or dominant member;
- expect conflict of views on the main issue and want to avoid it; and
- fear the consequences of making a decision.

As a result, the task is unfinished, the agenda is postponed, and the puzzled leader may wonder (during a sleepless night) what happened and what he might have done.

One leader might try—by exhortation, authority, punishment, or force—to make the members discuss the major issue. Another leader might indicate the clues he has observed and check whether anyone else has noticed them. Such a leader might suggest that members cease their flight from the major issues and discuss instead why they are avoiding the task. If this discussion is too difficult for the group to face openly, the leader might initiate a method to unlock the underlying problem: Each person writes his personal diagnosis of the difficulty on a sheet of paper and places it in the middle of the table. The sheets are mixed to shield identity and are then read aloud by one member.

By this procedure, the leader helps the group diagnose its own problem and legitimizes open group maintenance as an appropriate task. The members learn how to watch for clues to group dysfunction. and begin to take responsibility for their own behavior.

Member Impatience with Each Other

It is easy to sense when a group is on edge. Members speak more vehemently. Criticism and rejection of suggestions occur. Polarization and refusal to find a compromise are common. Subtle personal attacks creep into the discussion.

There are many causes for this situation: the group's dissatisfaction with itself; resentment at what is perceived as pushing by the leader; an emotional problem known to everyone but not dealt with; anger at one aggressive and overpowering individual. The group should be urged to tackle the basic issue troubling it. Here again, diagnosis followed by facing the underlying issue, whatever it is, should be the immediate task for the group. Only when leader and members realize the continuous interaction between "feeling facts" and "logical facts," and feel free to deal with that interaction, can a group work productively on the surface agenda.

Ideas Attacked Before Fully Expressed

When an issue has become polarized, or the group has divided into two hostile camps, statements frequently are attacked even before they are finished. Every suggestion is viewed as impractical. Different perceptions as to the meaning of the task or discussion method are present. No one listens fully to others. Cliques are formed. Hidden agendas of various members remain unexpressed but are revealed covertly.

When any of these situations occur, no progress will be made on the agenda issues until the underlying problem is brought to the surface. A leader may report that for the last twenty minutes no one has allowed another person to finish a statement. The leader asks, first, if others have noticed this (a few heads nod), and, second, what really is happening in the group. He may receive little support because emotions are high and most members are ready to do battle. The leader may then suggest that at least a speaker should be asked if he is finished and if he feels he has been heard. The leader may also suggest that each member, before responding to the previous member, paraphrase what he has heard the previous member say. If this suggestion is followed, the members might be astonished to see how poor listening can lead to serious misunderstanding.

Inactive Listening

Any observer can quickly note whether people are listening to each other. When there is little listening, the discussion flow goes in a jagged line, with each statement having only the most casual relation to the one just made. People give a variety of bodily clues. They may be leaning forward intently, with muscles tightened, waiting to break in with their own contributions. Where hidden agendas are present, each person listens only for the appropriate moment to introduce his purpose; his facial expression may even signal anger.

Listening is difficult. Each of us has a psychological screen through which we hear. This screen includes our aims and desires at the moment; what we think the person is saying based on our past experience with him; what we think of him and how much we like and respect him; what we think ought to be said about the subject; and a host of other experiences and emotions that add up to the stereotypes upon which we base our responses to individuals.

We are inside our own minds when we listen. We should be endeavoring to be inside the speaker's mind if we are to understand him. We should be listening for the dual messages in any statement—the music and the words. Perhaps the person is seeking status, support, love, respect, admiration. Perhaps he is communicating hopelessness and the expectation of failure in being heard and understood. Perhaps he is communicating hurt, anger, dislike, or provocation. Perhaps he is trying to become a more accepted member of the group by adding to the problem-solving process. Whatever it is, he is communicating *two* messages, and inattentive listeners may misread both messages. This is why real listening is hard work and full communication is rare.

Many leaders remain unaware of these complexities because their attention is solely on the task. The leader often naïvely assumes that everyone is dealing with the agenda issue. If he does recognize crossed communication, he may give his interpretation of what has been said as the correct one, instead of asking for clarification. Some leaders, on the other hand, strive to listen on both levels. They are aware that their own hearing may be inaccurate. Consequently, such leaders may paraphrase what they have heard and ask the previous speaker if that is what he meant and if he wishes to amplify his statement. They may even ask what motivated the member to speak. Such leaders try to become aware of the group's problems with listening. Leaders find that, when they model active listening, other members increase their sensitivity to the complex problems of communication. They find that members become aware that good communication is a joint enterprise between both sender and receiver.

Disagreement and Polarization

When disagreement and polarization occur, there is evidence either of conflict in the group, hesitation to deal with the agenda item, or fear that certain procedures are being suggested to block off discussion or give weight to the "other side." Interpersonal problems, fear of a powerful person, or fear of the consequences of any decision may be holding the group in an endless argument about plans and procedures that postpones or kills the main problem. Members may believe that any decision is irrelevant because someone higher up will nullify it.

Disagreement and polarization require attention to group maintenance, trying to turn a win-lose situation into a win-win situation in which no part of the group loses face by giving up. If the internal factors causing polarization can be solved, the group gains strength and cohesiveness. Frequently a polarized situation is presumed to be solved before the group has a chance to re-form as a group. A wise leader will spend time to insure that all members understand the issue in the same way and to discuss briefly some procedures to approach the problem. In this way, the group experiences a consensus, has time to feel a sense of being a group, and may be less likely to move into a win-lose stance.

Often, after an issue has become polarized, it ultimately is discovered that two sides are talking about two different issues under the unexamined assumption that they are dealing with the same issue. A leader, sensitive to such a situation, may urge the group to examine the assumptions held by various members.

Subtle Interpersonal Attacks

Antagonisms between two persons, carefully camouflaged to escape detection, may slow the progress of the group and create compromises that leave no one satisfied. Two clues can be observed. Who consistently speaks after whom may indicate a hidden conflict. A statement by the second speaker, such as "I agree wholeheartedly. However, I'd like to add an additional point" could be an example.

If apparently supportive but actually disruptive statements tend to occur each time Alice or Bob speaks, and before anyone else has had a chance to say anything, then the leader or members should sense a conflict. Someone, aware of the hidden conflict, may say for the good of the group, "I may be wrong and I'd like to know how others feel, but I've noticed that each time Alice or Bob speaks, the other immediately follows with a statement that doesn't seem to support the first. I wonder if Alice and Bob have some problem with each other they would be willing to talk about, with the hope that all of us could help."

There is no guarantee that either Alice or Bob will respond except to say that everything is all right. Both may be highly defensive, and the group, when the attacks are so subtle, cannot force the issue into the open. However, other members are now alerted to a possible cause for their group problems, and they will be better able to perform the task even with the submerged conflict.

Groups can also face equally subtle pairings in which two members tend to support each other, irrespective of the issue. Such pairing makes it difficult for the group to proceed, particularly if the supported statement runs contrary to the best thinking of the rest of the group. A cure to this pairing, if it is repetitive, lies in who talks to whom and who responds immediately. Eye movements can be watched unless every statement is addressed to the leader and all eyes are turned in his direction. If every time Alice speaks, she looks at Carol, and vice versa, it could mean that each is seeking the support of the other. It could also mean that a subtle antagonism is present and each looks to see how the other will respond. The type of response will help to determine whether the pairing reflects support or attack.

Discouragement

Sometimes a group feels discouraged with itself or feels it has no influence or power. The task may seem too difficult, the consequences threatening, interpersonal and intra-group problems unworkable. This discouragement is shown in many different ways. Sometimes it is expressed verbally. Sometimes a decision is delayed. Sometimes members slouch or are lackadaisical with discontented or faraway looks on their faces. Voices reflect feelings. Restlessness is felt in the room. Conversation drags and what participation there is runs at a low qualitative level.

If this feeling of discouragement or lack of involvement persists, or there is low expectation of results, members may arrive late, leave early, or be absent. There are prolonged delays in getting a meeting started because general conversation among groups of members is difficult to stop.

Some leaders, facing a discouraged group, may urge the members to stop work on the agenda item and endeavor to locate the causes of the discouragement.

The Hip-Pocket Agenda

Some members may bring hip-pocket agendas—purposes they wish to accomplish. Fully aware that announcing their agenda in the beginning would court rejection, they listen to the discussion with their ears attuned only for the appropriate time to disclose their purpose. It usually appears when a member with a hidden purpose says, "You know, I just thought of something that . . ." Seemingly off the top of the person's head comes the hip-pocket agenda, with the hope that it will appear spontaneous. Consider the number of possible hip-pocket agendas in any group and how much real listening to others has been going on. Then consider the difficulties in arriving at an adequate solution.

Entrance of New Member or Loss of Old Member

The manner in which a meeting responds to additional members or the loss of old members reflects the climate and strength of the group. If new members are ignored or their contributions rejected, or if the group shows undue discouragement with the loss of a member, the group becomes divided and loses its sense of being a group.

Sometimes a dependent group will toss its problem to the new member for solution. If he responds with a solution, he and his solution may be rejected because the answer does not meet the unsurfaced needs of the group. Or, if the newcomer's solution is accepted, the group may be saddled with a poor decision because the newcomer cannot know all the unsolved difficulties of the group.

If the newcomer is rejected or feels unaccepted, he may fight back by endeavoring to block future moves in the group. Or he may withdraw within himself, depriving the group of ideas that might have been of value.

Often a group will react with discouragement and depression when an old member leaves. There may be expressions that the group is now too small, lacks sufficient resources, finds the task too difficult. Here a leader or member needs to urge the group to examine realistically how drastic the loss is, whether others can fill the gap, and why the group is over-reacting.

Much broader than the prepared hip-pocket agenda are all of the possible hidden agendas individuals bring to a meeting or create at the meeting. These may include personal fears of the consequence of any decision; a need to conform to group expectations; a need for the leader's approval; relations with other members; feelings about competency in comparison with others; fear of rejection; or competitive needs or survival concerns.

The wise leader is attentive to clues of hip-pocket or hidden agendas. At times, members require confrontation regarding their unspoken issues. At other times, the leader will find a way to suggest an interpretation of the member's behavior to the rest of the group.

Rise or Fall of Noise Level in the Group

An obvious clue to group dysfunction is a change in the normal noise level. A rise in decibel level may well mean conflict between ideas, procedures, or interpersonal antagonisms. Lowering the level may indicate boredom, discouragement, and prevention of participation or involvement. A noticeable change in tempo may require attention from the group. Reporting this perception may focus attention on a maintenance issue. On the other hand, some increase in noise level may indicate the members' interest and excitement with their progress on the task. The alert leader can readily discover the difference.

Decision-Making Difficulties

Meetings have two separate difficulties with decision making. In one instance, a long list of relatively meaningless decisions are made in quick order with no dissent or questioning from members. The group members can leave, seemingly, with a sense of achievement. These decisions, however, will either be unimplemented, revoked, or brought up for re-decision at the next meeting. The real purpose of the group, in collusion with the leader, has been flight from the more serious basic issue.

In the second instance, a group cannot make a decision. Each time a decision seems imminent, another aspect of the problem is raised, and the group members settle back for further discussion. Usually the problem is postponed for further thinking or information, or a subcommittee is formed to wrestle with the problem. Obviously, there are times when a decision should not be rushed; when further information or study of consequences is required; or when subcommittee work is called for. These times usually appear objectively real. It is when a group consistently follows the same pattern that diagnosis and work on underlying problems is called for.

There are many more clues to potential group dysfunction. When the leader and members learn to think diagnostically about group behavior and to recognize that feeling facts are always present, they are acknowledging that a group has both task issues and maintenance issues. Both kinds of issues are important; they continuously interact with each other. Effective meetings require attention to both, especially when the group meeting is satisfying no one. By learning to deal with both task and maintenance, the group builds its strength to face future issues.

CHAPTER 4

CHARACTERISTICS
OF THE MATURE GROUP

To achieve maximum efficiency and high member satisfaction, group meetings need to strive for maturity through deliberate, systematic efforts. Groups do not grow haphazardly, nor is maturity automatic. Growth requires attention to group maintenance and time for strengthening the members' skills. Many groups, unfortunately, remain at an immature level because little effort is made to keep the group in good working order.

Group maturity involves growth in a number of dimensions. A discussion of these characteristics will indicate the kind of leader interventions and meeting methods necessary for productivity and satisfaction.

Involvement

The members in a mature group feel a sense of ownership— involvement in its task activity, group maintenance, and in the growth and learning of its members. Members feel that the group is theirs and that responsibility for its operation rests on all of them. While the leader has certain special functions to perform, leadership is shared by all. Group difficulties become everyone's concern.

In an immature group, the sense of involvement is fragmentary and there is very little sense of ownership by the members. The leader is expected to bear all the burdens of responsibility. Group failure is

Much of the original thinking and some of the characteristics listed in this chapter can be found in the *Report of the First National Training Laboratory on Group Development*, 1947, sponsored by the National Education Association and the Research Center for Group Dynamics, Massachusetts Institute of Technology.

viewed as the result of poor leadership that is unable to cope with diverse member behavior. This attitude deprives members of opportunities for significant contributions; and it tends to inhibit full expression of their ideas and feelings. In addition, by placing the leader in a dominant position, the members become passive followers who require directive leadership. This only confirms the common view that a strong leader is necessary to direct and control members in a meeting.

Responsibility

In a mature group, members assume greater responsibility for their own behavior and the impact of that behavior on both the task and their relationships with others. Members are more sensitive to the reactions and feelings of other members.

In an immature group, members assume little responsibility for their contributions to the welfare of the group. Self-oriented behavior is typical, with the clear expectation that control of disruptive personal behavior is one of the functions of the leader.

Trust and Caring

In a mature group, trust and caring among members allow them the freedom to express concerns, feelings, fears, and ideas. Trust and caring make it possible for members to reduce their defensiveness and accept and utilize the stated reactions of others to their behavior. In this way each member learns how he is perceived by others. As members increase in self-awareness and sensitivity to others, the group becomes more efficient, considering and using ideas from all.

In an immature group, more of a jungle situation exists. Most members fear attack from other members and hesitate to express their concerns and feelings. Striving for power and status threatens less aggressive members. Hostile feelings are not expressed openly but only in insidious ways. Weaker members mask their true feelings in order to placate and agree with dominant members and the leader. A pecking order develops, creating a distorted pattern of participation.

Use of Resources

In a mature group, diverse resources are sought out, accepted, and utilized. Conformity is sought only in the areas of trust, caring, and willingness to seek various ways of solving problems. Diversity of viewpoints is expected and allowed. Conflict is faced squarely by bringing conflicting purposes and points of view to the surface. And it is resolved constructively by the members working together for a creative compromise. Members do not fear either being different or thinking differently from others. No psychological uniforms are required. In this way a contribution can be examined, evaluated, and used without judgment of the person. Members also recognize that poor communication between two persons is a joint responsibility.

In an immature group, many resources are lost because they are neither sought nor accepted. Stereotyping of other members without attempting to examine the basis and validity of the stereotyping is common. As a result, many members fail to disclose differing ideas and opinions—the resources that any person brings to a meeting. Conflict becomes destructively interpersonal, and, while usually present, is seldom resolved because of the pretense that conflict does not occur in well-mannered groups.

Listening

In a mature group, listening is active. Individuals do not interrupt other individuals but endeavor to listen to their feelings and desires as well as to their ideas. Nondefensive communication occurs because there is less need for members to camouflage feelings and needs in devious ways. Emotions and differences are expressed overtly rather than covertly.

In an immature group, listening is a passive activity. Interruptions are common and misperceptions typical and frequent. Members are forced to find indirect ways of expressing their needs and feelings as well as their ideas. Usually there is a gulf between the members who are listened to and those who are not. Ideas expressed by certain members are accepted, whereas the same idea offered by another member is not really heard. Observing any group meeting will quickly disclose those who are listened to and those who are not—irrespective of the value of their contributions.

Self-Examination

A mature group is willing and able to examine its own operation with a minimum of defensiveness. Problems with the task, with methods of problem solving, with subgroup conflict, with interpersonal relations, or with disruptive behavior in the meeting become problems that the group tries to surface and resolve. If it is obvious that the group is not functioning well, the group diverts attention from the task and focuses on maintenance problems. Several diagnoses may be suggested by group members before the real problem is located. Through this process, members resolve a particular problem and acquire skills to respond to future problems. Members also learn to recognize and deal with similar problems in other groups to which they belong.

An immature group seldom deals with its internal problems; that is the leader's responsibility. Sometimes the problem—usually one dealing with the behavior of one member—becomes so irritating to the rest of the group that it is confronted in a brutal, punishing, and destructive fashion. This usually leaves a group more reluctant than ever to handle future problems, and a member who is hurt, angry, defensive, and still a problem.

Experimentation

A mature group is willing to be experimental with ways of observing and collecting information about its functioning or for the solution of its task. It may experiment with the temporary use of subgroups to collect data prior to full group discussion. The mature group tries different ways of using equipment, such as blackboard, newsprint, or tape recorders. Instead of accepting or rejecting ideas as they are expressed, they can be listed on the newsprint or blackboard—to be carefully evaluated and sifted later. It may try out different ways of planning the use of its time.

An immature group tends to be rigid and fearful of new ways of working. Usually the traditional meeting methods are set by the leader and remain unchanged, irrespective of the needs of the group. A "We've always done it this way" attitude prevails.

Using Subgroups

A mature group recognizes, accepts, and makes use of various pairings and subgroups that are based on mutuality of style, interest, and interpersonal liking. Such subgroupings are inevitable and can be integrated into the group. Subgroups and pairs can sometimes take on specific tasks for the rest of the group because the few who feel closest to each other may be best suited for a certain task.

Open recognition of subgroups or pairs prevents them from covertly manipulating the group. With such open recognition the group can also deliberately split natural subgroups to get the broader viewpoint that differences of approach, opinion, and resources provide.

Immature groups seldom openly recognize the existence of natural subgroupings within them. This deliberate blindness leads inevitably to covert influence and manipulation by a subgroup. Power blocs are created that weaken the chance of contribution by isolates—individual members attached to no subgroup. In turn, hostility and needless conflict between subgroups occur. Such covert subgrouping reduces the richness of diverse resources.

Dealing with Differences

A mature group takes time to explore differences in perception, need, purpose, and contributions of all members so that the group goal can include legitimate individual needs and utilize all possible resources. The beginning discussion of an issue may center on different perceptions of the issue, different expectations of outcome, different concerns, and different purposes, before the discussion zeros in on the solution. In this way, the members are clear about their different perceptions and understandings of the task.

An immature group seldom concerns itself with the perceptions, needs, and expectations of its members, but proceeds with the task as though all members view it in the same way or have similar expectations of results. In such cases long arguments end up with such comments as "I guess I misunderstood you" or, less politely, "I thought you knew what we were talking about," which inevitably lead to further argument.

Flight Behavior

A mature group recognizes the difference between flight from task and momentary rest or relaxation. Frequently, after one aspect of the task has been solved, or some group crisis resolved, the members will take a breather for conversation, anecdotes or a story, or a review of what has been accomplished. The mature group will be sensitive to the need for change in tempo.

A mature group also recognizes when it is in flight from its task—refusing to tackle problems, dropping agenda items, making decisions too rapidly, or talking around the subject. When it is clear that the group is in flight, the members explore the causes of the flight and seek to resolve the problem.

An immature group usually fails to recognize the differences between needed rest and flight. When rest is needed, the leader may attempt to drive the group back into a work mood, only to run into subtle resistance. In the case of flight, the immature group persists, with no attempt to seek the cause of its flight. The result is inadequate problem solving and decision making.

Accepting New Members

The mature group is able to incorporate new members and to use their resources. A mature group is sensitive to a new member's need to be included and views the new members as a potential resource. New members are accepted on their own terms and are not pressured to conform. The mature group recognizes that it will always be in a process of change, adding new members and losing old ones.

The immature group frequently resents the intrusion of an additional member, tends to reject or fails to use the contributions of the new member, and forces him to fight his way into the group. The result is usually the loss of a resource and the disruption of the group while the new member finds his way. His entrance may drive some present members into silence or create an interpersonal power conflict within the group.

Hidden Agendas

A mature group has learned to recognize and acknowledge that individuals may, from time to time, bring a hidden agenda to the group that they hesitate to share openly with the group because their agenda is so self-oriented. Members of a mature group have learned to allow the hidden agenda to surface in open discussion so that personal needs may be handled without disturbing or disrupting the group.

An immature group fails to recognize hidden agendas, fears dealing with them, and lacks the skill to bring them to the surface without punishment or conflict.

Hidden agendas occur because an individual or a subgroup believes that having such items will be judged as wrong, rather than as reflections of a legitimate need or purpose.

CHAPTER

TASK FUNCTIONS

Most groups exist to perform tasks. In meetings, the task involves information gathering, discussion, problem solving, making and implementing decisions, and evaluating the outcome of the group's work. Specific behaviors called *task functions* facilitate a group's completion of the task. In the leadership strategy described in this book, task functions are the responsibility of all the members, not just the leader. Shared leadership, as we have seen, makes maximum use of group resources and creates a sense of ownership and accomplishment for all who participate.

Critical in the performance of task functions is a sense of appropriate timing. Useful behaviors lose their value if they are premature, overdone, or are employed to thwart the progress of the group. For example, a periodic summary of the group's discussion can help the members to review quickly what has transpired. However, if a summary is offered too soon, it truncates the discussion and precludes further contributions. If the summary is made too long after the discussion has begun, points and opinions offered earlier may be lost. In another instance, the function of seeking information prevents premature decision making, but extensive fact finding and information seeking can postpone a decision indefinitely. The timing of task functions is an all-important skill to be learned by all who participate in meetings.

The functions described in the following three chapters were part of the research reported in the *Report of the First National Training Laboratory on Group Development* (1947) and were among the functions described in the classic article by K. Benne and P. Sheats, "Functional Roles of Group Members," in L. P. Bradford & J. R. French, Jr. (Eds.), *The Journal of Social Issues*, 1948, 4(2).

The task functions described here have been studied by many investigators of group behavior. Their evidence indicates that group meetings are most effective when the leader and group members share the responsibility for recognizing the need for performing these functions.

Developing the Agenda

An agenda is a list of topics or problems to be discussed; it provides an "order of service" for the group meeting. The method by which an agenda is developed is critical. Ideally, it should flow from all participants in the group meeting if a high degree of involvement and ownership is to be maintained. Traditionally, however, the leader builds the agenda before the meeting begins, or asks members to submit topics beforehand, or depends on reports from standing committees. This often stifles the productivity of the group. Instead, the development of the agenda can be the first activity of the group meeting.

Listing. The chairperson opens the meeting by placing a large pad of newsprint paper on an easel in front of the room. (Newsprint is preferable to a chalkboard because it allows a meeting to preserve all its discussion for later recording by the group secretary. It keeps a visual display in front of members at all times, so that the results of their work can be seen. The newsprint record provides a basis for reviewing the session at the end of the meeting. Having a visible agenda promotes group efficiency and prevents hidden agenda items from surfacing in the discussion.) Using a felt-tipped marker, the chairperson lists topics of interest to him, or items referring to leftover business. He invites the other members to state what topics they want to discuss and he writes their suggestions on the newsprint.

Setting priorities. When the list is completed, the chairperson initiates a brief discussion on which items to handle first. As the discussion proceeds, he numbers each item to show its rank order. This process of involving group members in fairly quick decision making on priorities sets the pattern for joint decision making on the items themselves.

Time Budgeting. The third task for the group is to determine how much time is to be spent on each item. Usually, the member offering an agenda item can indicate whether the topic is a "quickie" or whether it requires ten, fifteen, or thirty minutes of discussion. Rather than being rigid, time budgeting should be a tentative planning of the use of meeting hours. Otherwise, an inordinate amount of time can be spent on minor items while major issues are given brief attention.

By this time, the group has before it a list of discussion topics for which it has set priorities and time limits. All members can be prompted to share the responsibility of trying to abide by the time limits. Items can be checked on the newsprint pad as they are concluded. At the end of the meeting, the group can review the agenda to make sure all items have been covered. Members learn this agenda-building process quickly, and they frequently abridge the task by citing the amount of time they want when they announce the topic.

Initiating

The initiating function—the beginning contribution to a discussion—is vital at the beginning of a meeting and also when the group bogs down or needs to take up another aspect of the issue at hand. The original initiation is most effective if it comes from both the leader and one or more members. Later, as the group matures, initiation frequently is made by group members.

The original initiation from the leader may be substantive, methodological, or both. The leader indicates the chosen item on the agenda and gives whatever background is required before seeking opinions and information from others. Or he seeks opinions and gives suggestions as to how the discussion could best proceed, such as brainstorming of ideas, dividing into subgroups, etc.

Whether the leader's initiation is substantive or methodological, it is important that he immediately encourage the contribution of opinions and information by group members. This shared initiation is a crucial point in developing group involvement and member responsibility. If the leader fails to promote initiation by all members, the group can quickly become passive and uninvolved.

Initiation serves as the fuel for group movement. Without it, the group may drift needlessly. The leader and all members need to be sensitive to the appropriate timing for initiating further exploration or a new direction. The best way to do this is by inquiring about the group's need to move on. A typical initiating query might be "I wonder if the group has reached a point where we are ready to move on. I'd like to check to see how others feel, and particularly to see if someone still has a point to make on the issue we're now discussing. What do you all think?"

Information Seeking

Valid decisions require comprehensive information. Decisions can be narrowed and distorted by factors such as:

- Information is withheld because it is not sought.
- An issue is prematurely closed.
- Members hesitate to speak because they feel their ideas might be rejected.
- The leader indicates that he wants to end the discussion.

In many meetings, members reject or subtly ridicule the contributions of certain members who have low status in the group and, consequently, cut off possibly valuable ideas. The seeker of information risks the danger of rejection when the group is pushing for a certain conclusion, whether or not it is the best one. At this point the leader needs to be sensitive and supportive of a group member's actions. An appropriate comment from the leader can do much to legitimize member responsibility for carrying out needed group functions. Such comments might be "Shouldn't we examine this request for more information? It might turn out to be of help" or "Does anyone have any further information? Let's not close this discussion until everyone is satisfied that we have all the facts we need."

Information Giving

Giving information is obviously the counterpart of seeking information. This function illustrates the need for the leader to be equally conscious of the task problem and of the maintenance and development of the group and its members. The more information the leader can elicit from members the more he has helped them to develop responsibility for task functions.

Giving information can become a problem to the group when there is low trust, poor group cohesion, and disrespect among members. In such situations a highly competitive and aggressive individual can rush in to supply information before someone else has a chance. The more passive, noncompetitive, or insecure person, who might have supplied either the same information or further knowledge, gradually withdraws from group action and allows the dominating individual to be most active. Not only does the less aggressive person provide less information, but he also withdraws from fulfilling other group functions.

Although the amount of participation is seldom equally distributed in a group, a continuous disparity of participation is a sign that a few individuals have taken over all functions. Other members feel them-selves less and less a part of the group and, consequently, contribute less.

Opinion Giving

Opinions, like information, should be freely given in a group and each member should feel that his views, emerging from his experience, will be listened to. It is the group's responsibility to sort out opinions from facts.

The group's ability to carry out this responsibility depends on suf-ficient trust, caring and respect for each member, and active listening. The extent to which members interrupt certain individuals or sharply differentiate the attention given to them may indicate difficulty. In many groups, some members are never really heard—particularly their unspoken plea to be heard.

The leader, as has been indicated, has a major role to play in helping a group grow in responsibility, trust, cohesiveness, and qual-ity of listening. If the leader is active in encouraging better group growth and maintenance, some of the problems present in many groups can be minimized. The leader can judiciously bring detrimen-tal behavior to the group's attention.

Elaborating

Without elaboration, an idea that is only half stated may not be heard or used; and a potentially good idea may be lost. Frequently a timid and insecure member may present only a portion of an idea—like the tip of an iceberg. Another member or the leader may ask the original speaker to elaborate on his idea. Someone else may then expand on the idea. One of the leader's *group-building functions* is to listen for half-stated contributions and question whether the idea has really been considered by everyone or whether it needs elaboration.

The elaborating function has great significance for team building. Usually the more secure and aggressive members have less difficulty in presenting a contribution clearly and elaborating it if necessary. The more timid and insecure individual is the one who may need the most help in getting his ideas heard and elaborated. If he is passed by, his insecurity is confirmed and he becomes less active as a member, thus weakening the team. By ignoring half-stated ideas, the leader helps to create a group standard that rewards individuals who speak clearly and loudly and punishes those who need the most help and encouragement to become active and involved members.

Elaborating a point that turns out not to be useful does not, in any way, diminish the necessity to help elaborate any idea until its validity is thoroughly tested. Only in this way will each member feel he is truly part of the group.

Coordinating

Frequently two ideas presented by different members can be joined together, although at first sight they seem to have little in common. Rather than rejecting half of a total idea, the leader and group members should be sensitive to the need for bridge building. If coordination is not carried out at the appropriate moment, two separate ideas may polarize the group into two argumentative sections.

The leader who is aware of both task and maintenance issues views coordinating as a vital function; he accepts the responsibility of helping group members become equally aware of the importance of coordination and of the consequences when the function is not performed. By example, he assists and encourages group members to be sensitive to the need for coordination and skilled in bringing it about.

Evaluating

The important task function of evaluating needs must be performed with care so that *ideas* are evaluated—not individuals. An individual may feel that a critical evaluation of his contribution is a rejection of himself. Such individuals, unable to separate their ideas from themselves, may withdraw. Others may fight, creating polarization and conflict in the group.

To separate ideas from persons, the leader may suggest that the members list on newsprint all the ideas they can think of, without stopping to evaluate any idea. This brainstorming method makes the suggestions the property of the whole group. The members can then, as a group, rank the suggestions made. Gradually the best ideas are winnowed out, and members can see clearly that ideas are disassociated from persons.

A leader who is not so sensitive to the need for the separation of ideas from persons may use reward and punishment following a contribution, thereby keeping the members under his control and preventing a group from forming. Comments such as "That's a wonderful idea you had" or "Your idea seems way off the track" are equally unhelpful.

Energizing

Every group needs energizing forces to create movement. Energy may be provided by the introduction of a novel idea, a statement of feeling, some participative act that continues the momentum of the group, humor, or a short break. When a group is self-activated, almost every member is serving as an energizer. One mark of a self-activating group is the surprise members express that "Time has passed so quickly!"

Structuring

Procedures for structuring group discussion are obviously necessary for the development of the meeting. For many leaders and members there is only one structure set at the beginning and it never changes, regardless of the needs of the group.

Frequently, events in a group may call for a different approach to the problem. Opinions may be needed from all members or a dilemma needs to be resolved rapidly but fairly. In such an instance, the use of temporary subgroups may be useful. In different corners of the room, small groups of four or six might gather for ten minutes to collect members' thinking. Each group reports its results, preserving the anonymity of those who are fearful of speaking. In a short time the thinking of all the members has been collected without acrimony and the various reports can be analyzed for similarities or differences. As an alternative, the leader or a member might suggest that the meeting *start* with small groups collecting information about the problem before the whole group goes into a discussion.

Whatever the situation, a well-organized and mature group is able to be flexible about changes in structure and procedure during a meeting. For this reason, the function of structuring is extremely important to a group. Otherwise the group may become frozen in an inefficient or conflict situation. Either the leader or group members should feel free to perform the structuring function. In the beginning, it often is the leader who makes suggestions to help educate members, freeing them from rigid patterns by introducing different procedures and trying to explain how and why they can be used.

Effective leaders who believe in shared leadership educate and encourage group members to become sensitive to these task functions and to take responsibility for performing them. The more members share in group management, the less self-oriented behavior appears or is permitted by other members—and the more productive the group meeting becomes.

CHAPTER

MAINTENANCE FUNCTIONS

No one questions the time and cost necessary to repair and maintain the machines we use. Human relationships, infinitely more complex and variable, also require maintenance to keep them in good working order. The maintenance functions of a group focus on *how* the group pursues its task. These functions involve feelings, moods, attitudes, needs, and the growth of individual members and the group as a whole. In musical terms, task functions are the words of a meeting and maintenance functions are the music; both are needed for harmonious productivity. Like the task functions reviewed in the previous chapter, maintenance functions are the responsibility of all participants in a meeting—leaders and members.

Conflict, antagonism, lack of cooperation, and apathy are signs that maintenance functions are being neglected. The effective group, however, learns that consistent maintenance not only resolves problems; it makes working together a rewarding experience. A good group experience contributes to the growth of individual members. When members are clear about their needs and the group's needs, when they feel free to express those needs, and when their means of satisfying those needs are productive for the group, then they are fully involved in the group; they are able to help it develop into maturity. Such experiences enable members to become skillful and responsible group members, rather than merely being followers of a leader.

Gatekeeping

Gatekeeping is the function of keeping the group "door" open for the more timid, less talkative members to contribute if and when they wish to. This function may be carried out by the leader or any member who is sensitive to others' needs.

The amount of participation by each individual in most meetings varies considerably. Wide discrepancies may mean that some individuals would like to participate more but do not feel that they can for a variety of reasons—timidity, previous experience of rejection, inability to break through the loud dominance of a few, desire to stay out of a conflict, feeling that someone has already said what they might have said. If a member who had not participated in a meeting were interviewed after the meeting, he might say that he had nothing to say that was not already said. A little more probing might reveal that he did not think he would be heard or that he felt others might be impatient because he was a slow talker.

A person who speaks infrequently may sometimes lean forward with his mouth half open as if to speak, only to have someone else rush in with a comment. The silent member then closes his mouth and sinks back in his chair. The group loses a contribution that might have been helpful, and the member may experience personal inadequacy, buried resentment toward the group, or hostility toward the dominant members. This situation, which occurs in almost all meetings where more verbal persons dominate, reflects a problem of group maintenance. Effective group cohesion and growth require that members become sensitive to the pattern of participation in their group and aid each other. Although an individual may feel deeply involved in the discussion while remaining silent, it is important to know whether his silence stems from fear or choice. Acceptance and identity are enhanced by participation.

The gatekeeping function can be overdone. The individual member may have no desire to participate at the time or feel embarrassed when forced to say something. Perhaps he feels uninvolved in the current issue or truly has nothing to contribute. Careful observation of body cues—posture and facial expressions—as well as evidence of a long period of nonparticipation should precede any attempt to serve as a gatekeeper for another member. Gatekeeping should be done with vocal evidence of caring both for the individual and for the group. Otherwise, pressures for conformity can build up to a point where no member feels free to be natural in his contributions, and gatekeeping is used to produce guilt. However, sensitive gatekeeping is vital to good group morale; without it some members remain isolated and rejected, and potential contributions are lost.

Encouraging

Frequently, members need encouragement to participate in the meeting. Often an individual feels uncertain about the value of his contribution and presents a hesitating, poorly expressed idea that is passed over by more dominant members. If a member or the leader notices that the member's hesitation—rather than the quality of the idea—results in the point being ignored, he can give encouragement in a number of ways: by asking for elaboration; by restating the idea so that it is clear (with due credit to the originator); or by adding to the idea.

Frequently a leader can help to keep the group in good working order by calling attention to problems members may not perceive and by encouraging them to:

- Experiment with a new approach to a problem
- Change, temporarily, the meeting methods
- Dig deeper into the subject
- Explore new avenues to the goal
- Test ideas before making decisions

A leader can also serve the group by showing in a caring and concerned way, rather than in a punishing and demanding way, how members may help each other. As in all maintenance functions, sensitivity and watchfulness for clues are necessary so that the encouraging function is not overused.

Harmonizing

Frequently conflict may break out in a group over an issue, a plan for proceeding, or an interpersonal difficulty. Those members who enjoy fighting quickly take sides, polarizing the group. Those who have difficulty with fighting withdraw while the battle rages around them. They are loathe to enter the fray even to try to stop it.

The harmonizing function may be helpful in a conflict situation. The individual who performs this function seeks to find some common ground that both sides can accept, perhaps by locating a solution to the problem that is agreeable to all or by reminding the combatants of what is happening to the group—polarization with half the group on the sidelines. Members may then recognize that solving conflict by fighting is not a helpful approach to conflict resolution.

Harmonizing should not be confused with attempts to bury or deny conflict. Conflict in a meeting is inevitable; resolving it constructively is a challenge. Harmonizing is negotiation between opposing sides in which one member serves as a third-party peacemaker, trying to retrieve the best ideas of both sides. When overdone, harmonizing dulls the flash of creativity that confrontation can produce.

Consensus Seeking

During many meetings, issues become polarized, neither side will budge, and a win/lose situation develops. Consensus seeking is the maintenance function that can resolve the polarization.

In a win/lose situation, a group becomes locked into an either/or way of thinking, believing that one party must win and the other faction must lose. This competitive situation quickly deteriorates into a lose/lose conclusion. Those members who lose the argument can sabotage the winning decision by passively refusing to cooperate, by "forgetting" to implement the decision, or by storing up resentment to be used in future conflicts. The "winners" win the battle, but the "losers" triumph in the end. When competition and rivalry become intense, everyone loses.

Consensus means that every group member has an opportunity to influence the final decision. Members of the group reach substantial agreement, not necessarily unanimity. Consensus cannot be achieved by majority rule, "horse-trading," or averaging. Consensus frees the group from either/or thinking and emphasizes the possibilities of both/and thinking by focusing attention on needs and goals. In consensus seeking it is possible to achieve a solution that all members can regard as fair. When members strive for what is *best for all*, rather than trying to triumph over opponents, they fulfill the highest expectations of the democratic tradition.

Giving and Receiving Feedback

Feedback is a report of the impact a given behavior has on an individual member. It frequently takes the form of "When you said. . . , I felt. . . ," providing a check on whether the message received is in fact the message sent. Giving and receiving feedback is a maintenance function that provides a group with information about its progress.

Feedback is most useful when it is solicited, either by the leader or by individual members. Statements such as "I'd like to know your reaction to the problem-solving strategy we used this evening" or "I'd appreciate comments about the way I managed the time today. Did you feel rushed?" are invitations for members to critique the way things are done. This procedure allows comments on methods, rather than personalities.

Feedback is most effective when it is direct, specific, descriptive, immediate, and shared with the whole group. Giving and receiving feedback is a skill that has application in most interpersonal situations.

Standard Setting

The setting of standards is needed for both task performance and group maintenance. Occasionally the group needs to be reminded of its commitment to efficiency, fairness, and open communication. The person fulfilling this function can urge the members to deal with intra-group or interpersonal conflict instead of attempting to ignore its presence. The standard-setter can remind the members of the need for their trusting and caring for each other.

Periodically, the members may wish to discuss the norms or standards that are developing as the group matures. And if the leader is sensitive to both task and maintenance, then a standard that has emerged implicitly can be made explicit for future work.

Processing

The final ten minutes of a meeting can sometimes be reserved for a quick review, or processing, of how the meeting progressed. Individuals may volunteer to serve as observers during the session and then report their perceptions. This review can alert the group to its chronic problems ("We spent forty minutes discussing the budget, although only ten minutes had been allotted to it") and to its achievements ("For the fourth straight week, we ended on time"). As members become sensitive to this maintenance function, all can participate in review.

If face-to-face verbal evaluation and feedback is too difficult in the early developmental stages of a group, members can fill out simple forms rating the meeting and indicating what might have been done either by the leader or members to make the meeting more effective. These forms need not be signed, but can be read aloud, either at the end of the meeting for discussion, or at the beginning of the next meeting. After defensiveness has been reduced, a group can move to a verbal evaluation. After this stage, immediate reactions and feedback during the meeting become more possible.

In any meeting, task functions will be more prominent than maintenance functions. But maintenance is no frill. Without attention to moods, feelings, and interpersonal relationships, a group chokes its lifeline of energy and motivation to complete the task. As maintenance functions become second nature to members and they become skilled at diagnosing group problems, teamwork is strengthened and working together produces the satisfaction of a job well done.

DYSFUNCTIONAL BEHAVIOR OF GROUP MEMBERS

Dysfunctional, self-oriented behavior results when groups fail to perform maintenance and group-development functions. When little attention is given to overt and covert problems—and then only by the leader—members feel little responsibility for the group. The session becomes the leader's meeting—not the group's—and in one sense, no real group exists for individual members. The tighter the leader controls task functions and a few group functions, the greater the amount of dysfunctional behavior in the group. Conversely, when the leader shares responsibility and helps members learn how to control and develop their own group, there is less dysfunctional member behavior.

When an individual perceives himself as alone in a collection of individuals, he is likely to push for his own hidden purposes and seek power and status at the expense of others. He may develop fears and dislike others who appear threatening; he may seek a few other members with whom he can line up for mutual protection; he may readily stereotype others on the flimsiest evidence; or disrupt the progress of the task for his own ends. When individual needs and purposes are not accommodated within the group, persons may either withdraw to the psychological shelter of silence or actively pursue their purposes without concern for the feelings of others. This is particularly true when no standard of group concern is established by the leader. Then the stage is set for clique formation and competitive struggles for power.

A sensitive observer quickly becomes aware of the many ways in which individual behavior can disrupt group progress, either directly or indirectly. Because most meetings have unstated norms that prevent the basic needs and purposes of individual members from being revealed openly, individuals find covert ways of expressing their true needs and feelings. Bouts of pseudo-logical argument, thinly veiled hostility, and an increase in the noise level (as if the loudest were the best argument), whirl around the group without touching the basic interpersonal or personal issue. The result is a ragged, time-consuming meeting without value to anyone.

COMMON DYSFUNCTIONAL BEHAVIORS

Some common dysfunctional behaviors are discussed briefly here, followed by suggestions for how a group-centered leader might handle them.

Blocking

Blocking involves interference with the progress of a group by going off on a tangent, arguing too much on a point, or focusing on irrelevant details. Blocking halts and derails the meeting from the track of successful work.

The person who blocks discussion may be unaware of his motivations, or he may consciously block to express his antagonism toward the leader or other members. The blocking member achieves momentary power by focusing attention on himself, rather than on the issue.

Power Seeking

When a group's structure is based on a hierarchy of power and status, the door is open for members to do all they can to gain more power in the group. Power seeking is seen most clearly in conflicts with the leader or other power figures. To gain power, individual members may try to create a clique of followers, thus splitting the group. Subtle ways of twisting a decision or trying to appear as the major force in a decision also reflect power-seeking activity.

Some leaders fight to hold on to their authority, but there is danger in becoming involved in an open fight with power-seeking members. When this occurs most of the group members withdraw from the struggle and remain quiet, while two or three do battle. Then the group disintegrates as an efficient working force.

Recognition Seeking

When a member draws undue attention to himself by talking excessively, advocating extreme ideas, or behaving in an unusual manner, he is seeking recognition. Often, after a statement is made by someone else, the recognition seeker will add an example or repeat in different words what has been said. He may divert the discussion with a meaningless anecdote in which he is the center of the tale. His comments are usually self-centered although he may endeavor to attach them to the flow of discussion.

Some leaders find such recognition seeking hard to control. Other leaders, who have helped develop the group's maintenance skills, trust that recognition seeking will be handled in a straightforward, tactful manner by group members.

Dominating

Loud voices, definitive pronouncements, and endless speeches from members often dominate the discussion and consume valuable time in some meetings. The dominating behavior of one or two members can prevent other, less forceful members from speaking out; frequently, it produces a tense, combative atmosphere. Members who dominate are usually insensitive to the needs of others and are unaware of their impact on group members.

Special-interest pleading is another form of domination. Many meetings are plagued by the speeches of members who lobby for their own favorite projects and insist that their problems be dealt with first. Such lobbying introduces superfluous issues into the meeting and has the same impact as blocking and dominating behavior.

Clowning

Clowning and joking give a meeting an atmosphere of play rather than work. Work need not be serious, and occasional comic relief can lighten any group discussion, but persistent joke telling and remarks that contain veiled hostility disrupt a meeting's progress.

Many other behaviors—silence, denying, polarizing, seeking sympathy or attention—can be dysfunctional in a meeting. Although such behavior may reflect the personalities of individual members, it is more useful to regard these behaviors as symptoms of inadequate group maintenance which prevent the meeting from operating at its best.

CONFRONTING DYSFUNCTIONAL BEHAVIOR

The leader can confront dysfunctional behavior by following these general guidelines:

- Confrontation is most effective in a caring context. Confrontation is an invitation for an individual member to examine carefully his behavior and its consequences. It is a way to express care and concern, not punishment. If the group has built a level of trust and commitment to group maintenance and team building, confrontation will be seen as a helpful activity. The case examples in the following chapters indicate ways in which dysfunctional behavior may be confronted.

- The leader should focus attention on the dysfunctional behavior itself and avoid labeling or classifying the person. Personal labeling only increases individual defensiveness.

- The leader should point out the effects of dysfunctional behavior. Often, the person who is interfering with group functioning is unaware of the negative impact of his behavior.

- Alternative behaviors should be suggested that will lead to more productive, satisfying participation for the disruptive member—and the rest of the group as well.

In confronting dysfunctional behavior, the leader models a direct, firm, but friendly style that group members can emulate. The confrontation alerts all members to watch for the occasions that call for group maintenance. As a group develops into a team, all the members will want to keep the communications lines open and the group's task in clear focus.

CHAPTER

THE EFFECTIVE LEADER IN ACTION

Effective leadership is shared leadership. In previous chapters, the task and maintenance functions that the leader shares have been described and the characteristics of the mature group have been noted. Methods have been suggested for diagnosing critical situations in group meetings. A way to confront dysfunctional behavior has been outlined. In all of these discussions, the leader's understanding of mutual responsibility provides a basic theme: shared power and authority increase group ownership and involvement, which in turn heighten the productivity of the group and the satisfaction derived from being a participant.

It is time to take a look at the effective leader in action. The narratives that follow describe a series of different meetings illustrating the group-centered approach.

Case 1: Starting a New Group

■ Increasing juvenile delinquency, senseless destruction of property, and the changing pattern of youth activities are beginning to concern the citizens of West Medina, a small middle-class community. These changes, which seem unrelated to racial or poverty problems, prompt the mayor to look for the causes and seek solutions. He names a committee to make recommendations on youth problems and needs. The committee of about twenty members is composed of persons from various community organizations, schools, churches, business, labor, courts, and police. The chairwoman, Dorothy Arnold, is a well-known, respected member of the community acceptable to all the different groups. The committee is known as the Committee on Youth Activities for West Medina.

Because of their previous experiences with unproductive meetings, the prospective members of this group arrived with some suspicions about this new committee. They needed to be convinced that this group would be worth an investment of their time and energy.

■ All the appointees are present at the first meeting, although a number of them privately plan to see how things progress before they decide to continue as active members. They do not want to belong if the meetings become a battleground between agencies. The chairwoman opens the meeting with a short speech that includes the following ideas:

This committee does not have an easy task, and it cannot please everyone. In order not to add a divided committee to the other problems of the community, the members should face and work through any conflicts they have. They share the responsibility for the committee's task, and the vague description of that task requires the committee to be flexible in meeting the problems that arise.

Because the task extends over an indefinite period of time, it could be weakened by four events:

1. Members might easily tire and quit because a strong and exciting group is not developing.
2. Members might make quick decisions, without adequate information, in order to satisfy the organizations they represent.
3. Members might postpone making decisions out of fear that they are not making the right ones.
4. Conflict between agencies and competition for power among members could weaken the committee's productivity.

These possible dangers need not occur if the members will work together to build a strong committee. Because the members represent different organizations and diverse viewpoints, they undoubtedly can provide an excellent variety of resources.

There is a great deal of experience and wisdom among the committee members, but the committee lacks first-hand knowledge of the feelings of young people because none are on the committee. Planning *for* young people is more difficult than planning *with* them. The chairwoman concludes by explaining her attitude about her own role:

"I do not have any answers and I hope no one expects me to resolve these problems alone. I see my function as helping the committee become a hard-working group in which we respect each other and explore and use the group's resources wisely. I see myself as a servant to the group, not as its director."

In this brief introductory statement, the leader described her understanding of the task, expressed her own concern about the group's productivity and stated some reservations she had about the committee's membership. She clearly indicated her own position and her intention to share responsibility with the group. She attempted to delineate the functions she would perform.

■ Dorothy begins the meeting by separating the group of twenty into four clusters of five each, sitting in different parts of the room. She asks each cluster to make two lists to share with the total group. The first list is to include what they think are the major problems facing the committee. The second list is to include problems that might keep the group from working at its best—problems that could interfere with progress. Suggesting half an hour as enough time for this task, she says she will check with each group periodically to see how much time they need.

The chairwoman's introduction was realistic. Although Dorothy warned of the difficulties the committee might face, she hoped that trust would begin building immediately. She rejected the customary round of introductions because they are used by some people to establish status, and may be so long-winded that everyone becomes bored before they get around the group. The task was deliberately chosen so that no single problem was tackled. Two agendas were constructed: (1) an inclusive list of task problems with no ideas rejected; (2) a list of group problems to alert the members and set a standard of openness about group maintenance difficulties. (If the group had started on a problem right away it might become polarized.) By getting the committee members immediately involved, a number of tasks were initiated. In the small clusters, the members could experience success because everyone's ideas would be included. This experience could help to weld the group together.

Through the use of small clusters, quicker introductions could be made and a broad list of problems would be gathered. At the same time, Dorothy started the members thinking about the need to become a group and sensitized them to potential maintenance issues. Thus the dual mission of any group —working on task problems and working on maintenance problems—was initiated.

■ At the end of the time period, Dorothy checks to see if the two lists are completed and asks each cluster to report its findings. She has two easels of newsprint in the front of the room. On one she lists the community problems that each group has discussed. There are obvious duplications reported by several clusters, but the composite list seems to represent the thinking of all the clusters and, it is hoped, of all members.

On the other newsprint pad, Dorothy lists the internal problems foreseen by the members. As might be expected, there are fewer of these because members are not familiar with the subject and many hesitate to indicate all their concerns. Concerns that do appear on this list include the following:

• The representative of an agency might push the particular viewpoint of that agency.
• The committee might bog down into conflicts over partisan viewpoints.
• Panaceas for particular problems might be forced on the committee before full reflection is given to the problem. Certain well-known members might endeavor to control the rest of the committee.

As Dorothy lists the members' concerns, she comments that although other problems will probably occur from time to time, the members are now forewarned of some problems they may be able to handle or avoid.

The newsprint provided a visible summary of the small groups' discussions. Clearly, developing the agenda was a collaborative effort that promoted ownership of the meeting by all members. By attending first to the list of potential maintenance problems, Dorothy indicated that she viewed maintenance functions as vital.

■ Dorothy then turns to the other list, commenting that it contains immediate and tough long-range problems—problems that require a lot of information before even tentative decisions or conclusions can be reached. She suggests that the group review the list and indicate which problems are of immediate concern and which should be delayed.

Setting priorities for the agenda promoted interaction among members and made them aware of the relative importance of the problems and their own readiness to deal with them.

■ After deciding on the agenda, the chairwoman asks each member to introduce himself, mentioning his name and the organization or agency he represents. She explains that after working together in the cluster groups, the introductions will now have more meaning. The committee members accept this proposal, briefly introducing themselves without evidence of status building.

Permitting interaction prior to introductions allowed members to get acquainted as persons without roles or stereotypes.

■ The first meeting ends after the introductions are completed and a regular meeting time is established. The members linger for a short while to chat with each other.

The chairwoman noted the noise level and the fact that no one left immediately. These cues told her that the members were involved and felt free to voice their opinions.

■ At a subsequent meeting, the committee is in danger of being polarized over an issue. Certain members of the committee are taking stands that their associations or agencies always take. Argument and counter-argument are exchanged, with no one serving in a bridging or coordinating role. Although the arguments are couched in mild words with considerable rationalization, Dorothy recognizes the problem. Because group members have begun to perform a few maintenance functions, she waits to see if some other member will comment on the situation. She concludes that this situation is a little too hot for a member to handle and she decides to intervene.

The leader, who had been observing closely, picked up the cues of group dysfunction, but she did not rush in. Instead, she gave the members an opportunity to share the leadership. When they did nothing, she modeled a maintenance function.

■ A pause in the discussion gives Dorothy a chance to say that one of the problems the group had anticipated is occurring: pressures from outside organizations are operating on some members and in the meeting. She expresses understanding of the loyalty felt by members toward their parent organizations. Then she suggests that instead of debating the two ideas being presented, the members find some relationship or a bridge between the two opposing ideas. A few heads nod and the discussion swings to a search for a third position.

By focusing on how the task might proceed, rather than taking sides in the argument, Dorothy helped the members build their problem-solving skills. She sanctioned organizational loyalty but focused attention on the work of this committee.

■ At a later meeting an issue arises that seems to require information, or at least reactions, from the youth of the community. A couple of members state that if decisions are to be made on the basis of information rather than prejudice or stereotypes, they should talk to young people. Although other members agree, they also feel that young people might say what they believe the committee wants to hear. Some members question the value of hearing the opinions of a few because all youths do not think alike.

The chairwoman observes that the group seems to be polarized over the issue with no one offering an alternative. Both sides want information from youth, she says, and they need to discuss a method of obtaining it. After a few comments, the committee begins to discuss how to get information from youth.

Dorothy resolved the polarization by noting that it was means, not ends, that divided the group. She clarified issues and then urged them to work on how to obtain the information they want.

■ The committee meetings continue. Members show growing sensitivity to group needs and are becoming skilled in performing necessary maintenance functions. Then, the atmosphere in the group suddenly begins to change. Instead of interest and energy, the members seem to be apathetic. With fewer members contributing, participation drags. Disagreement and nitpicking are prevalent. The discussion wanders away from the issue before the group. After the meeting has dragged on for awhile, the chairwoman reports what she is observing and asks the members if they want to pause and talk about what is happening. There is dead silence for a moment or so, then a few mild assertions that everything is all right. Then Dorothy asks why their behavior during the last two meetings has been so different. Someone suggests an answer: they are a little tired. The chairwoman says the change in behavior seemed to occur when they tackled the present agenda issue; perhaps there is a connection.

One member states that for him the issue seems vague and he does not know where to catch hold. Another wonders if they are wise to discuss the issue now. This triggers another member to say that he is afraid that any decision they make will lead them into trouble. Other members speak, making it clear that they all are concerned about the consequence of any decision. They worry that others in the community will misunderstand whatever they do.

The chairwoman suggests that if this is not the right issue for this group, probably they should not tackle it. Despite their feeling of responsibility to carry out the task assigned to them, perhaps the timing of this issue is inappropriate.

The leader reported the clues she observed and confronted the group with her observations. She invited them to report their feelings and fears about the decisions to be made. By sanctioning discussion of their personal feelings, Dorothy saved the group from a monotonous, unproductive period.

■ In a later meeting, one member, Joe, blocks the rest of the group just as they are making some progress. Although no one has said anything to Joe, Dorothy senses the tension mounting in the group. She is uncertain whether Joe realizes that he is holding the group up, or whether he is clear about his own motives. She speculates that he believes he is helping the group to consider all possible points. Finally, Dorothy tells Joe that when he stops the group from reaching a decision, everyone seems to get tense, and she also feels blocked when he asks the group to reconsider too many points. She asks him if that is the message he wants to send out.

Dorothy gave Joe straight feedback, reporting the impact of his behavior on her and the members of the group. She asked him to clarify his message.

■ Joe responds that he has no intention of blocking the group. Then several members say that although they also had felt that Joe was blocking them, they had assumed Joe had a good reason for his actions. Dorothy suggests that Joe might summarize periodically for the group to make sure they are covering all points, thereby providing a service for the group and assuring himself that all points are heard. In this way, Joe's needs would be met with the sanction of the group.

The work of the Committee on Youth Activities continued. In the committee, the chairwoman was an effective leader because she viewed her leadership as a service to the group—the service of sharing responsibility and helping to increase the satisfaction of the members with their collective task.

Case 2: Evaluating the Meeting

■ Fred, the new administrator of an organization, has been in office for four months. There are no crucial problems demanding immediate attention so he observes and listens. He senses that persons throughout the organization are apprehensive that he might make drastic changes affecting their work. Intentionally, he makes the first staff meetings similar to those conducted by his predecessor.

When Fred senses a reduction of tension in the organization, and then notes a number of disruptive and competitive forces operating in the staff group, he calls a staff meeting and takes the first of a number of planned steps. Toward the close of the session, he suggests that the group review its functioning. He asks the members how they feel about the meeting and what might have been done to improve it. There are a few moments of silence, broken first by one person and then another who assure him that the meeting had been fine and they could think of nothing to change. No one adds anything and the leader closes the meeting.

At the next meeting, Fred tries again. This time he seeks reactions to his own behavior, although he doesn't expect many responses. However, he sees his action as a model of how the group might work later. At the end of the meeting, he says "There was a place, which I'm sure you will recall, when my comments seemed to freeze the group (and he describes the incident). No one said anything at the time, but you can help me now by telling me how you felt about what I said."

A few individuals assure Fred that what he said was perfectly all right and no one felt blocked. Because the other staff members remain silent, he has no way of knowing how they feel. Although no helpful reactions result from his efforts, Fred feels that by asking for feedback, he may free others to begin to do the same.

The next staff meeting follows the previous pattern. There is little response that is not positive. This time the leader questions the quality and consequences of the decisions made and asks if any member still has an idea that has not been expressed, but nothing is said. Explaining that it is impossible for him to be aware of all that is happening, he asks the staff to accept responsibility for expressing their ideas, although they consider them of little consequence. It is the responsibility of the staff to judge the usefulness of an idea; its rejection is not a rejection of its originator.

At the fourth staff meeting, some progress in evaluation is made. One member, quickly seconded by another, mentions that the group has wasted quite a bit of time on an unimportant side issue. Although the person who has led the group astray says he feels the side issue was important, most of the group does not agree. Fred says that the group is making progress by bringing up such problems. Otherwise any individual with good intentions can slow up the group.

He asks why the group waited until evaluation time to bring up an issue that must have been seen earlier by some members. What could have been done at the time to change the direction of the group discussion? Considerable discussion reveals that some members feel no acceptance or mandate to interrupt the group and question what it is doing. Others fear an interruption might hurt someone or cause conflict. No one knows how to break in without sounding domineering.

Seeing this as a good time to help establish a group norm, Fred suggests that a description of what is happening in the group might be useful from time to time. Such a statement would prompt discussion in the group.

Each meeting thereafter shows progress in group evaluation. At some meetings members fill out a short reaction form, leaving it unsigned. These are shuffled and read aloud to start discussion. Other problems appear: how to support each other, how to get wider participation, how to inform some aggressive members of others' feelings. At one meeting a member describes another organization in which every six months most of the professional and administrative staff devote an entire day to examining carefully the problems between groups in the organization. The group considers this procedure worth a try, but decides to try it out first before involving others in a wider meeting.

The leader was aware that he had to move slowly. The major task he faced—to build a staff—was not entirely dependent on him. As a first step in improving the organization, he wanted a staff group that could confront and handle its interpersonal and group problems. This could best be achieved by helping the staff learn to evaluate its performance regularly.

Case 3: Confronting Conflict

■ The leader of a small committee is plagued by a compulsive talker and by two persons in a head-to-head conflict. The chairwoman talks to the three persons in private, but with no results. When she tries to bring the discussion back to its original purpose, her efforts are continually disrupted by their behavior. Clearly, the three individuals are so self-oriented that they are insensitive to the impact of their behavior on others.

At the same time, no other member of the committee considers it his responsibility to deal with the disruptive behavior. The group lacks skill in dealing with such problems while avoiding more conflict.

After two disastrous meetings, the chairwoman decides to bring problems to the surface, and by her own behavior show members how to solve future problems. She intervenes in the next meeting after an argument between the members who are in conflict. She says:

"I'm not certain how the rest of you feel, and I would like to check your reactions, but for the past half hour most of us didn't participate at all. Alan, you and Margaret took up much of the meeting time and I wonder if there is an issue between the two of you. Could the rest of you state how you feel about these arguments and their impact on the rest of the group?"

Alan says he hasn't noticed any lack of participation and, furthermore, he and Margaret are friends. They would not intentionally disturb the group. Margaret nods her head. Another member says he thought Alan and Margaret had some kind of battle going on between them, but he didn't know how to break it up, so he remained silent. A few others indicate their agreement.

To prevent an argument with recriminations passing back and forth between Alan and Margaret and others in the group, the leader intervenes again. She says that two individuals may become so engrossed in an issue that they can forget the rest of the group; this is natural and not a cause for blame. What members should do is remind such a pair of the impact of their behavior on the group.

These statements by the leader relieve some of the tension in the group. One member says she is uncertain how to give feedback without being critical. She also wonders how a person avoids being hurt or defensive when someone confronts his behavior.

The leader admits this is a problem. For feedback to be useful, there must be a lot of caring and trust in the group. Such caring and trust develop, she says, as the group has successful experiences in working together. They do not develop for those who remain silent and bottle up their anger, or for those who talk too much and do not listen to others. Perhaps, she says, if a group member checks his perception of what is happening with others rather than making a flat charge, the group may develop a non-defensive climate.

After more discussion about making the group more effective, the leader suggests they return to the committee's work. Although Alan and Margaret are silent at first, they soon become involved in discussing the task but with much less of their previous rivalry.

After the meeting, the leader asks Alan and Margaret how they feel about the meeting and particularly about the feedback they received. Both say they are glad to know how the group feels. The leader is not certain they mean what they say, but she has tried to help them release their feelings.

The leader realized that the only effective means for controlling disruptive behavior was by the group members themselves. By modeling interventions, the leader taught group members without becoming the permanent controller of their behavior. She checked her observations with others, and prevented an atmosphere of punishment. She indicated the need for trust and caring to develop and helped the group to see that every successful experience they had would make the next problem easier to face.

Case 4: The Classroom Group

■ Leon, a fifth-grade teacher in an elementary school, realizes that trying to teach individual children is not half as effective as trying to build a group in which children learn to take responsibility for helping each other learn. Of course, the teacher recognizes differences in intelligence, competence, interest, and personal security, and he knows many educators believe that competition for rewards often motivates learning. But Leon believes that, in the end, internal motivation makes more thoughtful students. He is also aware of the destructive consequences of failure for individual students; being at the bottom of the class seldom builds a sense of self-worth.

He finds that when children help other children learn, they

augment their own learning and also build social skills. He knows that when struggling students receive caring help from their peers, it increases their motivation to learn and their sense of self-worth. In addition, if a class becomes a group with a feeling of oneness, all students help each other.

Leon is aware that he might be trading individual competition for group competition if his class feels superior to other classes in the school. He plans to help the children be more concerned with their own growth and learning and less concerned about being better than another class. By helping the children base their behavior on intrinsic motivation, he also is helping them gain greater internal strength and increased awareness of their own identities.

With these principles in mind Leon plans his program. Fortunately the desks in his classroom are not attached to the floor. Leon asks the students to sit on cushions in a circle around him. He talks about the friendship and fun they can have as they work together. He explains that if any one of them needs extra help or is having difficulty, another child can try to help—everyone can help someone else. They will spend every Friday afternoon sitting in a circle, talking about how the class is doing and about any problems they have in learning or in their relationships with each other. During the afternoon they can talk about anything that is disturbing anyone or the group. He welcomes any suggestions that will help him be a better teacher and helper to the group. He wants them to feel like a big family.

At the first Friday afternoon meeting, he asks if anyone is having difficulties with the subjects the class is learning. A couple of hands go up. One child says he does not clearly understand their work in arithmetic; in fact, he is beginning to feel lost. When the teacher asks if anyone feels sure of himself in arithmetic, several hands go up, and a student volunteers to help the child who is having difficulty.

On another Friday, a problem emerges concerning the relationship of two children. Leon encourages the rest of the children to talk about the problem and find ways to help the two.

The Friday meetings continue, and the children look forward to them. They become more willing to talk about their problems and to accept help from other children. They seem to like each other more, feel more like a group, and their school work is very satisfactory.

One day when Leon has to leave the room for a time, he asks the children to decide on the details of a picnic planned for the following Friday afternoon. He says this will call for some leadership. When he returns, he sees two of the strongest leaders clustered around one of the most timid students, one with fewer experiences of success than most of the other children. Leon discovers that the two strong students, rather than struggling for leadership, influenced the group to choose the timid child as their leader. Now they are engaged in reassuring and helping him.

A week later Leon asks the timid child how he feels about the class and school. The boy says he has never been happier in school in his life. He seems more sure of himself, his school work has improved, and he needs far less help from other children. His overly dependent and subservient behavior has begun to disappear.

As time goes on, the children seem happier and Leon's earlier concerns about the emotional well-being of a few children disappear. Although the children are not equally competent, no child feels failure—nor should he—in terms of his accomplishments in learning. The sense of self-worth grows for all who are in need of it. Many social skills are learned. The children are more sensitive to others and seem to care for each other. They learn how to give help and are more tolerant.

The teacher, believing that a strong, caring group could increase the learning of all, worked to build a group out of separate individuals. By so doing, he not only increased their competence in the curriculum subjects, but helped the children gain in social skills and personal security.

Case 5: Group Standards or Norms

■ A condominium composed of twelve town houses forms a semicircle around a beautiful park area. All the residents are retired or semi-retired couples. Their children are grown and living in other parts of the country. Grandchildren often become the topic of conversation at parties or when two couples meet for an evening. There is a considerable amount of neighborliness. If the wife becomes ill, the other families take turns bringing a hot dinner to the husband. When any couple goes on a trip, others watch the vacant home and collect mail from the local post office. Over a couple of years a sense of closeness develops. Although the residents come from different parts of the country and from different occupations, these differences become less and less important.

Someone suggests at a party that they have a weekly discussion group to talk over issues of the times. There is some approval of the idea, but enough silence to table the idea. It is clear that some couples feel they have a disadvantage in terms of background; others are not really interested.

However, the idea is brought up again and it looks as if a group might get started. One couple, the Bennetts, have had considerable professional experience with groups of all kinds and they are disturbed about the dangers involved. Arguments can break out, leaving part of the group ostracizing the other part. Stereotyping is such an easy habit that some persons might be labeled according to their religion or politics.

The Bennetts finally decide to share their professional knowledge and concern with the others, hoping that the discussion group might avoid some pitfalls. Drawing up a list of possible guidelines they want to talk over with others, the Bennetts invite their neighbors over for an evening.

Mr. Bennett starts the conversation by saying that he and his wife think a discussion group will be stimulating, but it might be well to talk over the idea before plunging into it. The feeling among neighbors in the condominium is warm, caring, and wonderful, and they hope it can continue. Different backgrounds and experiences represented in their group offer tremendously rich resources to share with each other. This is extremely valuable, but, he says, it goes beyond the limits of reality to expect that all will agree on everything. If everyone thinks the same thing, they cannot learn from each other. Differences, unfortunately, might create arguments—not discussion—and divide their small community. Argument can lead so easily to pinning labels on each other rather than listening and learning from each other's point of view and knowledge. It would be too bad to disturb the good feeling the residents now have. Then he asks Mrs. Bennett to present some guidelines they are suggesting for the discussion group:

- We need to accept each other for what we are, and try not to judge each other when we don't agree. We need to hang on to our liking for each other, no matter what.
- We should listen for interesting points of view that we all can explore, rather than reject ideas.
- We should present our ideas and opinions as just that— opinions. The greatest danger any of us face is thinking that we are *right*.

- We need to listen carefully to each other—a very hard thing to do—and try not to interrupt.
- Each of us is an expert on something, and none of us is an expert on everything.
- We should all express ourselves. If some of us say nothing, we will quickly dry up discussion because only a few will talk.
- Women have something to say—encourage them to say it. The idea that only men know about the larger issues of the day and women know only about the home is old and sad. It keeps some women from entering into a discussion and some men from really listening to them.
- Each of us should monitor his own participation so he neither monopolizes the conversation nor sits back and says nothing.

After Mrs. Bennett finishes reading the points, a discussion starts. One person suggests that people avoid talking in an authoritarian tone of voice. A few modifications of the list are made and most people express pleasure about the guidelines.

The group then concentrates on topics for discussion. Someone suggests they start talking about the experiences they are having with retirement—as individuals and as couples. This will certainly pull the women into the discussion because they probably have strong feelings about retirement that may be very different from the feelings of the men.

This idea is accepted as the first topic. When someone says the group should keep away from religion, another agrees, but adds that it might be valuable to talk about what life means at their ages. Someone suggests that they look at some of the problems of the day, and another wants to talk about young people and their ideas. There seems to be no dearth of things to talk about.

Someone suggests—and all agree—that the Bennetts should act as discussion leaders. The Bennetts agree to serve for a few meetings and then see if someone else will take a turn.

The Bennetts were concerned about all the possible problems faced by a discussion group starting with no planning for the process of the group. They thought the best thing they could do was to help those involved establish some standards or norms of individual conduct and group action before the group started.

CHAPTER

USING A CONSULTANT

Task, maintenance, and team-building functions are the joint responsibilities of all who attend meetings. At times, a group or organization may want to call in an additional resource—a human relations consultant—to assist in building and strengthening its skills as a work group. The human relations consultant brings special expertise in group functioning to the organization's meetings and also provides an outsider's perceptions of the group. The task of the outside consultant will vary with the needs of the organization, but generally, he provides observations, collaborates with group members in diagnosing troublesome areas, and teaches and models a variety of useful skills. The consultant is temporary help. After helping members to learn, and to increase their sense of group ownership and involvement, he departs.

Hiring an outside consultant is part of a long-term process called organization development. The case history that follows describes how an organization used the services of a human relations consultant over a period of time to increase the effectiveness of its meetings.

A Case for a Consultant

■ George, the president of a small company, presides over a decision-making group of vice presidents and department heads. Although he tries to be an energizing force for his employees, he is aware of conflict and other difficulties each time his group meets. George begins to wonder how to solve the group's problems and he decides to hire a consultant. He asks the consultant to help diagnose the organization's difficulties and to build a sense of group ownership among his staff.

The Consultant and the Contract

■ The consultant, Colleen, has a long talk with the company president, who describes the situation as he sees it. In addition to George's concern with the in-fighting in the group, he also is troubled about his future. In his early sixties, George has a health problem, and a part of him wants to retire; another part of him is reluctant to release power and uncertain about who should succeed him. George's ambivalence has the top management group in a state of confusion, anxiety, and competition.

Colleen explains to George that she sees herself as working for the entire staff and not just for him; she intends to make that clear at the first meeting. And, in order to open the door for others, she will elicit feedback from the group about his behavior. Although it would be natural for him to be defensive in front of his subordinates, she adds, this might prevent the members from ever opening up. To help the members communicate more openly, she suggests that, at an appropriate time, George invite feedback from the group.

The consultant says she plans to observe a regular staff meeting, but first, in order to develop some trust and get acquainted, she would like to have a personal interview with each member of the group. The president agrees to her request, and Colleen feels that she has established her own ethical contract with him.

In negotiating her contract with George, Colleen indicated that she perceived her task as working with the entire group. She did not intend to provide a smokescreen for George but, rather, would treat him as she would treat all members of the group—fairly and candidly. The personal interviews would help her to understand the situation better and to begin a relationship with all the members. Colleen realized that this was asking for considerable trust from the president, but she felt these requirements were necessary so that others wouldn't see her as the president's "hatchet man." As it was, she faced a difficult task in winning trust from others.

Personal Interviews

■ Colleen's interviews with the management personnel reveal quite a number of disturbing problems. In addition to the weekly meeting that all attend, the president meets regularly with each half of the group—those with line authority and those with staff responsibilities. Although no one questions the wisdom of having separate meetings, many express concern, even some anxiety, that they never really know what occurs in the meetings of which they are not a part. Almost everyone indicates that two vice presidents—one in finance and one in sales—are competing to be president of the company. In addition, several members report a considerable amount of covert competition among all departments. There are some cliques, but their members do not entirely trust each other.

Colleen also wants to interview a sample of employees who work under the department heads, but their selection presents a delicate problem. She does not want to interview a subordinate who will merely parrot his superior, nor does she want someone who feels animosity toward his boss. To solve the problem, she asks each department head to name three or four subordinates from whom she may choose at random.

These interviews provide Colleen with a variety of responses, including many that substantiate the statements made by department heads. She gains a number of insights about the department heads, including the extent of their worry about how they and their departments stand in the eyes of the president, and the antagonisms that exist between areas and departments.

The Staff Meeting

■ At the meeting of management personnel that Colleen observes, she notes that the president vacillates, sometimes calling on individuals when discussion lags and sometimes remaining curiously quiet; he is quiet at crucial points when group members feel the need to know what he is thinking. Participation is uneven and some individuals remain quiet during the entire meeting. Although always on a covert level, the conflict between the two vice presidents becomes more obvious as the meeting progresses. Some members seem to be totally uninvolved, while others become quite tense and active when certain issues come up. It is clear that no decision becomes final until the president ratifies it. When he remains quiet, the item is left dangling.

The consultant completed her data collection. Thorough fact finding is necessary when the members of a group have many interrelations with each other. Satisfied that she was beginning to know the organization fairly well, Colleen now prepared for a major intervention.

The Schedule

■ Colleen is scheduled to hold three three-day meetings with the management group at four-month intervals and away from the office. Her goals are to build greater team-work among the individuals and to solve some of their conflicts. Between the three-day events, she also plans to observe some of the weekly management meetings.

Team Building: First Meeting

■ The first meeting is held at a retreat center some sixty miles from the office. All who attend are expected to stay overnight throughout the event. In opening the meeting, Colleen, now fairly well known to all, expresses hope that the meeting can be very informal. She repeats her contract—that she is working for all, not just for the president—and her assumption that the company is "owned" by all of them, not just by the president. Her interviews and observations have indicated that the president feels—and acts—as if the weight of the entire company is on his shoulders alone. Others seem to feel and act the same way about their departments and areas. The consultant questions whether this makes for good working relations, and she hopes the group develops its sense of oneness as the meetings progress.

Colleen presents a list to the group, synthesizing her interview results and other observations. Each item is a problem mentioned by a number of individuals. She has printed on a large newsprint pad on an easel the following:

- Problems of competitiveness
- Uncertainty as to the president's retirement plans
- Feelings of need to protect one's department at staff meetings
- Disenchantment with the meetings
- The president's silence at crucial points in the meeting
- Uncertainty about how the president values and rates each department

The agenda item, "silence at crucial points," draws the first response. Because this behavior leaves individuals uncertain as to what the president wants or is thinking, they are also uncertain whether to take action. Remembering the consultant's warning about defensiveness, the president asks the group to remind him of their needs at such times. He explains that:

- He often is caught between feeling that he is dominating the meeting and wishing others would speak up;
- The times he is most quiet are when he feels guilty about having been too active;
- He is eager to hear the ideas of others when he is silent;
- He has been unaware that his periods of silence bother the group and he hopes they will alert him to their feelings in the future.

The consultant suggests that the group improve its communication by letting the president know when his reactions are crucial, but not so often that they become completely dependent on him to ratify or reject every point. The president asks them to remind him both of when they need his reactions and when he might be shutting off their ideas. There is little reaction from the members, but Colleen feels some relaxation of tension. Furthermore, she feels that she has shown them one way in which they can work more effectively as a group.

The next problem discussed is concern over the two separate group meetings the president holds each week. Some complain about their lack of knowledge of what goes on in meetings they do not attend. Admitting that he has not been very sensitive to people's feelings, the president says he thought that everyone knew each group had different problems to discuss. The consultant comments that whether or not people ought to have concerns about what is being discussed in the other group, the fact is that they are concerned.

This is obviously a problem for the total group, and a long discussion follows. One member suggests that there be only the one meeting. Another suggests that the meetings be held less frequently with more issues brought to the total group. Some other members define the issue as basically one of trust. They don't mind two meetings as long as they feel confident that:

- Any issue involving them is made known to them;
- Their department is not subject to discussion without their knowledge; and

- They are kept abreast of decisions affecting the company—and thus their department.

No decision was made at this point but the issue of trust was now firmly before the group and could not be avoided. As the consultant's interviews of subordinate employees disclosed, the lack of trust and the competition and anxiety in the management group was well known in the organization; this reinforced the necessity to look at their problems. Although the issue of trust could not be avoided, the group discussed it gingerly and rather intellectually as if the problem really was not theirs. But Colleen felt satisfied that with the issue on the table they would inevitably come back to it many times and in different ways.

■ The problem of the intense competition between the two vice presidents has not been discussed openly as yet, although it affects the whole group. Circuitously someone approaches the problem with a delicate question to the president, conveying concern about when he is going to decide about his future. The president responds that he is consulting with the Board of Directors of the company and, of course, it is their responsibility to name his successor. No one in the group really believes that the president does not have either the final say or a great deal of influence in the selection of the new president, but the inquiry is carried no farther. However, the consultant feels that every probe is a step toward the members taking more responsibility for the entire company and for the development of their group.

During the free hours of the conference and in the relaxed atmosphere of the retreat center, there are many side conversations between group members. One or two members seek out the consultant for a brief talk on ways they might approach a problem in their own department.

By the end of the morning of the second day, Colleen senses that the group has gone as far as it can at this meeting in exploring its own problems. So she suggests that, as an experiment to test how much progress they have made as a group, they tackle some major company problem—but not one that puts a burden of blame on any individual.

The group gladly accepts this suggestion. With the president now serving as leader and the consultant as a silent observer, they list a number of overall problems, including some long-range changes in product development. The discussion carries over into the evening, with the latter part of the evening devoted to looking back at how they have worked. When the consultant asks members how they feel, she is pleased that some individuals say they feel freer to express their own thoughts without worrying so much about what the president thinks.

Colleen then adds her observations. She has noted wider participation than in the earlier meeting. Contributions are being made in a less authoritarian manner, and there seems to be more listening. Contributions are less self-seeking or department-oriented. Having noted the president's attempts to bring in a couple of silent members, she evaluates his efforts as thoughtful but also slightly punishing, something she doubts he is aware of. She asks the members concerned how they feel. They are somewhat reluctant to answer but do admit that, while they are pleased with the president's concern, at the time they did not have much to say. Colleen then demonstrates ways of inviting others to participate when they choose to, and helping others to feel comfortable in the group.

The first three-day meeting, ending early in the afternoon to allow time to drive home for dinner, is completed with a leisurely conversation on reactions to the meeting and on general suggestions for ways in which they can work together most effectively. Colleen and the president review the meeting. The president says he has learned a lot and he thinks they have worked out some of their problems. He has some new reorganization thoughts as a result of this meeting. The consultant feels that real progress has been made in developing the group, and she hopes they will be able to tackle some of the deeper problems later.

Weekly Management Meetings

■ Colleen observes at least one weekly meeting during each of the ensuing three months. At first, she sees some effects of the three-day meeting: in wider participation, increased efforts of department heads to work together, and greater efforts on the president's part to see that decisions in various meetings are communicated to all. Although the consultant feeds back observations about the group from time to time, as the months progress it becomes clear that there is some regression to an earlier stage of fear and competition. Even so, several members talk to her about how they are doing in the group, or ask how they might handle a problem with another department head or in their own department. Gradually members of the group are becoming more aware of the delicate problems in human relations and in group behavior.

Team Building: Second Meeting

■ The second three-day meeting begins with a totally different mood and atmosphere than the first one. The consultant feels more trusted and accepted. Without developing any agenda, the group opens up a discussion of the rivalry between the two vice presidents. Various members of the group state that while they like and respect both men, they feel they are expected to show loyalty to one or the other. This they do not want to do; such pressure is bad for the company.

A break comes when one of the two rivals says that, although he feels competent and wants the position of president, if the choice goes the other way, he is prepared to guarantee his loyalty to the other vice president, who is also competent. In addition, he suggests that they both might talk about future planning for the company so that if either secures the position, there will be initial accord. He promises to initiate such talks. The other vice president responds that he feels the same way and welcomes talk between them.

Because the president's retirement is naturally a part of this discussion, George says that he has had long conversations with members of the board of directors and a final decision will be reached at least by the next three-day meeting.

Several other conflict areas, between departments rather than persons, are discussed. In some cases there are mutual recriminations, but the consultant always intervenes by asking whether they are trying to resolve the problem. This usually triggers third parties to help solve the issue.

Several members talk about their efforts to improve relations among those in their department and particularly to improve their own staff meetings. This interchange of information about beginning efforts to improve their own departments and to talk openly about conflict among their subordinates—competition of which they had been largely unaware—is, in the consultant's opinion, a major step toward trust and openness in the group and identification with the group.

Colleen observes that group members, without always being aware that they are doing so, help the group on both task and maintenance levels. There are fewer remarks with punishing overtones. There is more respectful listening and less interrupting of each other. As these improvements appear, the consultant makes the group members aware of what they are doing and how.

As the consultant observed them, the weekly management meetings between this three-day conference and the last one were better meetings. Group decision making was based on wider participation and more thoughtful and company-oriented thinking. Openness and collaboration among members had increased with a consequent reduction in hidden agendas and subtle verbal attacks. The consultant was aware of greater relaxation on the part of the president—he no longer felt that he was carrying the entire load of the company.

Team Building: Final Meeting

■ The final three-day meeting is fascinating. A decision has just been made by George and the board of directors that George will now become chairman of the board and the vice president who made the initial statement of loyalty will become president— although this is not the reason he was selected. With the encouragement and help of Colleen, this three-day meeting is largely devoted to talking through with the new president how he sees himself working with the group and how the members want him to work with them. Nothing is done at this meeting concerning any plans the new president might have for the company because there has not been time for him to formalize any.

Essentially, the group occupies itself with re-forming as a team under new leadership. The consultant thinks to herself that few presidents, or leaders in any organization, have the same opportunity to form a good working team at the very beginning of their tenure in office.

Some time is spent in examining the progress various supervisors have made with their staff. Some groundwork is laid for a more extensive organization improvement program for the entire company, although no plans are formalized. The meeting ends with a review of the group's accomplishments over the year.

Reviewing the Consultant's Work

From her interviews and observation, Colleen readily arrived at a diagnosis that the first task was to help build a strong, cohesive, trusting management team. Without such improvement and understanding at the top of the organization, little could be done to improve the rest of the organization. Her findings indicated clearly that the president's practice of carrying the whole load of worry about the company was emulated by vice presidents and department heads, carrying the same worry for their units—an action that, in turn, encouraged nonproductive competition among them. The result reinforced the president's insularity. This circular process of reinforcement was at the heart of many of the company's problems, including the president's hesitation about retiring. The consultant realized that the process of building a strong, effective group took time and called for delicate efforts. So she took the following steps:

- She collected information by interviewing members of the group and a sample of their subordinates. Information they had supplied not only fed into her diagnosis, but also made it harder to avoid or reject.
- Realizing that the initial behavior of the president would be crucial, she discussed her plans at length with the president, cautioning him not to expect instant miracles, and stressing the necessity for him to be as nondefensive as possible.
- She opened the first three-day hideaway meeting with the group by stating firmly that she saw herself working for the group and the company and not for the president.
- She expressed the hope that the group would come to feel that in a psychological sense they "owned" the company—it was not owned only by the president—and for this to occur, the members must become an effective group.
- By presenting a synthesis of her interviews and observations, Colleen brought into the open problems that all the members were aware of but had not been able to discuss. She was able to present the problems neutrally to the group and the president; if any progress was to be made, these problems would have to be dealt with.
- After the group discussed the first problem—one dealing with the president's actions—and after the president indicated willingness to accept help, the consultant suggested ways for the group to help the president. By doing so, she provided concrete ways for members to take on necessary group functions.
- By the second day, Colleen had gained some trust and the members were assured that she was not there to force actions upon them. In a leisurely fashion and with no pressure, she could

discuss some very simple, basic ways in which a group could take more responsibility for its own actions.

- During the next two meetings, as members began to carry out group functions (often without realizing that they were doing so) she pointed out what they had done, helping them to learn more about performing task and maintenance functions.
- Through modeling, she showed the group how to evaluate its own activities, discover problems it had not dealt with, and find ways of working more effectively.

Using a human relations consultant to help develop an organization can be extremely useful, especially in times of crisis. Many different kinds of organizations can benefit from the interventions of an "outsider."

CHAPTER 10

GIVING A LARGE
MEETING THE QUALITIES
OF A SMALL-GROUP MEETING

Leaders of large meetings face major challenges in attempting to provide participants with the following experiences:

- Active participation in making decisions
- A sense of personal achievement
- Face-to-face communication
- A chance to express their ideas and otherwise contribute to the group
- Person-to-person working relationships

In small groups (20 members or less) many persons feel freer to share their ideas, problems, and feelings with others. As individuals communicate directly, they get to know each other and stereotyping decreases. Decisions or solutions evolved in a small group are felt to be the accomplishments of each person, and consequently, are more closely defended and implemented. Feelings of trust, caring, fellowship, and friendliness are more readily developed in a small group. Competition among cliques and subgroups becomes rarer as the size of the group becomes smaller.

A variety of methods can be used by leaders of large meetings (more than 30 members) to foster the qualities found in small groups.

Case 1: The Situation

■ In a large city hospital, rumors have spread that a decision has been made to stop overcrowding the hospital with patients from outlying areas and to expand facilities in nearby satellite hospitals. Naturally, these rumors have caused many of the hospital's staff to worry about their jobs, although the staff has been complaining about the overcrowding for a long time. However, although the idea has certainly been in the minds of many people, no decision has yet been made.

The superintendent of the hospital is concerned about the disruptive effect of the rumors. Wishing to include the hospital staff in any decision made, he plans the first of several meetings. Aware of the traditional distances between the staff roles—doctors, nurses, dietitians, paramedical personnel, housekeeping and maintenance staff, and administrative personnel—he anticipates that each will react according to his position. Therefore, the superintendent sees the need to secure thinking across professional lines as well as the thinking of each group.

Case 1: The Meeting

■ The first meeting is held in a large room at the hospital. Although chairs are originally lined up in rows facing the front of the room, they can easily be moved around later. As he faces the rather large group of people, the superintendent senses their anxiety and fear. He tells his audience that no decision has been made about decreasing the load in the hospital by increasing facilities in nearby smaller hospitals; nor will one be made until the staff of the hospital has a thorough chance to think through all sides of the issue. The danger, he says, is in acting on the basis of panic and fear. Then he recommends a plan for that day's work.

During the morning, following the superintendent's recommendations, staff members meet in small groups according to their similar hospital roles. Each group compiles three lists: (1) advantages to the hospital if regional hospitals are expanded; (2) disadvantages that will be caused by the change; and (3) changes that will be required if the final decision is to go ahead, and possible barriers to these changes.

Toward the end of the morning, the superintendent asks a representative of each group to copy the group's three lists on sheets of newsprint that are taped to the wall at separate spots in the room.

After lunch, different groups are formed, this time cutting across professional roles. The superintendent asks some of these groups to examine the lists of disadvantages as objectively as possible to see if the problems can be overcome without damaging the services of the hospital. He asks other groups to examine the lists that contain required changes and possible difficulties and to suggest ways to handle them.

At the end of the afternoon, each group is given an opportunity to report its thinking.

Some of the morning groups are violently against any change in hospital policy. They see any cutting back of the hospital's work as the first step to the ultimate destruction of the hospital itself. To them, any change will lower the hospital's reputation.

Other groups are positive, seeing expansion of the satellite hospitals as a way to decrease the overload of work for some staff members. Most of them describe difficulties to be overcome if a change were made. As expected, groups that are most opposed to any change also see more difficulties to overcome.

Reactions from the more heterogeneous afternoon groups are also varied. Of the groups examining the reasons against change, most are able to ameliorate the most negative reasons and they find some ways in which certain functions of the hospital can be strengthened while regional resources are improved. Other groups, seeking ways to handle barriers to change, find that certain compromises can be made.

At the end of the afternoon, the superintendent asks if sufficient thinking about the problem has taken place. As he expected, the staff wants to study the problem further at one or two more meetings. The superintendent agrees but asks a favor of those present. Naturally, people in the same role—doctor, nurse, etc.—would tend to talk among themselves. He asks that each person make a real effort to talk with someone outside his group and bring to the next meeting a wider understanding of how others feel and why. This might prevent the freezing of opinions before everyone has a chance to think the problem through.

Lastly, the superintendent distributes the following questionnaire and asks everyone to fill it out anonymously:

1. To what extent did the way the meeting was conducted make you feel a part of the discussion and decision-making process?

   Very much　　　　Some　　　　Little　　　　Not at all

2. To what extent were the groups asked to work on the most important and relevant issues?

   Very much　　　　Some　　　　Little　　　　Not at all

3. To what extent did you personally enjoy this type of meeting?

    Very much　　　Some　　　　　Little　　　　　Not at all

4. Would you prefer that the superintendent and his cabinet make the final decision without any further consultation with the staff?

    Yes　　　　　　No

5. Please write any further comments you wish to make.

The superintendent was pleased with the results of his brief questionnaire. Most people liked the way the meeting was conducted. Some sheets contained such comments as "First time I have felt a part of the hospital"; "The meeting went more quickly than any I've attended here"; "Whatever decision results, at least we will feel a part of it." There were some negative comments, such as "Waste of time"; "Decision already made and this was just a show"; "An effort to brainwash us." But on the whole, the responses were highly favorable and indicated great involvement in the problem.

The superintendent himself was uncertain of the best answer. But he was sure that the entire staff had to be involved in considering the issue. If he, or his small cabinet, were to make the decision alone, the repercussions, possible sabotage, and loss of crucial staff would be a bigger loss than the time taken for consideration and discussion by the entire staff.

The Diagnosis

Far more important than the organization of a large meeting into small groups is the leader's diagnosis of the crucial issue and whether the use of small groups is helpful in dealing with this issue.

In the preceding case, the superintendent was aware of a number of underlying forces in the hospital and, consequently, he knew what he had to accomplish. He knew of the rumors and he could understand the fears of certain staff members that their jobs would be lost. He knew that most of the staff believed that he and a few top officials had already made the decision. For these reasons alone, it was imperative to have small groups of people talk among themselves and consider as many reasons against a change as for a change. He knew it was also important for the groups to look realistically at barriers to change, as well as at ways to overcome the difficulties. Finally, he believed that having small groups give their reports in public would dispel the idea that decision making in the hospital was done behind closed doors.

Case 2: The Situation

■ A children's home is established in a community as the result of a wealthy woman's gift of a large house. About a dozen children are brought there to live under trained supervision. The children are either somewhat retarded or have emotional difficulties.

Although the children cause no trouble in the neighborhood, a few people wish to close the home thinking that it is bad publicity for that neighborhood and it reduces property values. A few articles and letters appear in the local newspaper and a special meeting is held by the town council, but the few protesters cannot arouse enough support and the issue gradually dies down.

Later, word spreads throughout the community that two houseparents who are living together are not married. They had been assumed to be married when they were hired at the children's home.

With this knowledge, the issue explodes once again. Some people, outraged that the houseparents are not married, join with the original protesters in urging the closing of the home. Others, who believe that the two houseparents are doing a good professional job and are not harming the children in the slightest, see no reason why the laborious task of finding equally competent professionals should be undertaken again.

The story is picked up by newspapers in various parts of the state, as well as in nearby states. Editorials published in some papers are damaging to the reputation of the community, and this outside publicity only hardens the attitudes of those on both sides of the issue.

The mayor of the community avoids the argument because he sees himself losing votes, whichever side he takes. His attitude is shared by members of the town council. When passions rise to the point that legal suits and countersuits appear likely, the mayor feels he must take action. He thinks that an open meeting of citizens might air the situation; then a small group can be chosen to reach a solution. He asks the high school social studies teacher to conduct the meeting because the teacher is well liked in the community and has a fine reputation as a discussion leader.

Case 2: The Meeting

■ The teacher opens the large meeting by stating what he perceives his task to be. His role is to remain completely neutral on the issue of the children's home, while helping the citizens work toward a solution of the issue. He says the greatest danger lies in splitting the community into two warring camps whose hostilities might endure for many years. Believing that no one wants to hurt the community, he hopes the healing of the community will become the real issue.

Outlining how he wishes the meeting to proceed, the teacher presents two issues for discussion: existence of the children's home is one issue and peace in the community is the other. Assuming that the issues cannot be solved in one meeting, he feels the spirit of the first meeting and the way people work in it will determine the nature of future meetings.

He asks the participants to form circles of six to eight persons. Each small group is to come up with suggestions for solving the issue of the children's home without hurting the community. Although each small group will contain people with different opinions about the issue, the emphasis should be on reaching a harmonious solution. The small groups will give everybody a chance to speak out and contribute to solving the issues.

When part of the audience expresses reluctance to try this new method, the teacher says that individual speeches on the issue will lead to a stormy meeting and will polarize the community, leaving neighbors not speaking to neighbors. For the good of the community, the experiment is worth trying, he says. If it does not work, people can still make a fight of it.

This last appeal persuades many of those present, although there is still grumbling and two speeches are made by two persons most actively representing different sides of the issue. The teacher listens calmly to their statements, but before more can be made, he points out that these two speakers, well meaning as they may be, prove that more speeches will do just what he feared—further heat up passions. Everyone knows, he says, how each side feels. What they have not done is explore how the problem can be solved without hurting the community.

The groups are slow in forming, with some individuals taking the initiative while others hesitate before joining a group. Finally, all are in some group. Discussion starts slowly, but gradually it picks up momentum as evidenced by the increasing volume of sound. After about an hour and a half, the leader recognizes by the decrease in sound that the discussion is slowing down, and he stops the groups. He suggests that each group choose a representative.

The leader has the group representatives form a semicircle in front of the audience. He questions each representative about the thinking of his group.

Some groups discussed only the issue of the children's home, from one viewpoint or the other. A couple of groups adamantly demanded legal action, both pro and con. But a good number of groups did seek ways of reaching a peaceful solution. Their suggestions included getting a statewide legal decision on children's homes, collecting information about how other communities handled similar situations, finding another facility in another part of town, and they even considered putting pressure on the couple to marry quietly without any notoriety in order not to affect the children. There were suggestions for planning further meetings, and for forming a joint committee composed of some members for the home, some against, and some who are neutral but committed to a healing solution.

After all the representatives have reported, and the audience has responded, the leader urges a decision about the next step. After much discussion from the floor, a committee is formed to consider all the suggestions and points of view expressed and to come up with at least two plans of action. These plans will be presented to another public meeting in two weeks' time.

Although not certain, the leader feels that the goal of preventing longlasting dissension in the community has been accepted and that even the most vociferous advocates will not venture to take any steps for the next two weeks. The meeting has at least temporarily defused an explosive situation, giving more influence to the moderates who serve as a third force.

The Diagnosis

The leader was extremely perceptive in recognizing that the most serious issue was prevention of a harmful and lasting division in the community. By using small groups to work on ways of saving the community, he prevented the more enraged speakers from inciting the citizens. If he had asked the small groups to come up only with arguments for and against the home, the use of small groups would have done nothing to help the large meeting.

Case 3: The Situation

■ During the summer, the new president of the women's church group gives much thought to how she can develop better monthly meetings. She discusses her goal with the chairwoman of the program committee. Both are aware that although attendance at the luncheons and meetings has been good, it usually takes some urging by telephone to make sure that certain individuals attend. They know that some individuals attend in order to be seen. They also are aware that the meetings have not changed in format or style over many years and that some of the younger members are voicing dissatisfaction outside the meetings.

The chairwoman consults with a group facilitator, an expert on meetings, who happens to live in the community. She suggests that an informal leader be placed at each luncheon table to help the women participate more fully in the meeting. When the facilitator offers to spend a half day helping the leaders prepare for the meeting, the president and chairwoman eagerly accept. In selecting the leaders for each table, they choose women who are sensitive and helpful but not domineering.

The purpose of the half-day training program is to show the leaders how to encourage participation by all and to discourage anyone from dominating the discussion or deriding or rejecting an individual's suggestions. By appropriate questioning, the leader should be able to bring the discussion back to the issue and make certain that everyone at the table has a chance to participate.

Using a flip chart, the facilitator writes a few sample questions or comments the leaders might make, such as the following:

- "Don't we want to get ideas from everyone before we decide which ideas seem most practical to us?"
- "I'm curious about what Mrs. Smith thinks will help our organization."
- "I think we were told that we have only a limited length of time, so wouldn't it be wiser to go over each suggestion first before we have any prolonged discussion on one suggestion?"
- "As I understand your point, Mrs. White, (cutting into a repetitive speech) aren't you thinking that. . . . Perhaps we can discuss your idea briefly so that we'll have time to consider other suggestions."

After considerable discussion about how the informal leaders can help the group rather than lead it, the facilitator suggests that they practice some of the ideas. There is time for about three role-playing scenes, with plenty of time after each one for evaluations of how the "leader" handled the situation. When the half day ends, the chosen leaders express tremendous relief and new confidence that they can help their groups.

The letter announcing the first meeting of the year promises a surprise and a speaker of considerable local reputation.

Case 3: The Meeting

■ The first luncheon meeting is well attended. To make certain that longstanding cliques will be broken up and that each table will have a mixture of old and new members, the president places name cards at each table.

Before luncheon is served, the president announces that she and the program committee are asking the members to take a new look at their church group. What should the organization be like? What should it do? What kinds of meetings should they have during the year? Having talked to a number of members, the president is aware that opinions differ on what the organization should be like. She says these differences are very natural but they demonstrate the importance of finding an organizational policy that will meet a variety of interests, rather than merely continuing old patterns. The president poses three questions for members to discuss at each table:

1. What kinds of programs or speakers would they like to have for meetings during the year?
2. Should the organization involve itself in some of the community's social problems—youth, drugs, schools, the poor—and, if so, what kinds of programs would be most relevant for their organization?
3. Is a luncheon meeting once a month just right, too frequent, or too infrequent?

At the end of the luncheon, just before the president introduces the speaker, she asks one person from each table to report the thoughts expressed at that table. The chairwoman of the program committee records all the ideas for her committee to consider later. The president promises to report to the membership with a proposed plan based on the ideas expressed by the groups. Then she introduces the speaker, who congratulates the president and the organization on reviewing its purpose in such a unique way.

The Diagnosis

The president sensed a growing split between old and new members that could have led to the ultimate decline of the organization. She used small-group methods to involve all members in deciding what kind of organization was best suited to them in changing times.

These cases have indicated how, after an adequate diagnosis of the basic problems, small-group methods can be used in large meetings of almost any size (if space is available for many small groups) to involve members in the decision-making process. Otherwise, decisions are usually made by a small committee or by a few dominant persons at the large meeting.

THE SPECIAL PROBLEM OF SPEECHES, LECTURES, AND SERMONS

Traditional speeches, lectures, and sermons are designed to inspire and inform those who listen. The speaker contributes by imparting his message, whether in a speech to an organization or convention, a lecture to a university class, or a sermon in a church. But the listeners are passive, contributing only their listening—all too frequently partial. The speaker is producing. Audience members receive. The very word *audience* denotes listening and hearing rather than participating and doing. Audience members expect to be informed and inspired, but not to act. This attitude becomes a barrier to change or action on their parts. A psychological distance exists between them and the speaker.

Members of an audience seldom have ways to respond or collaborate with the speaker. As a result, they react by either identifying with the speaker, admiring his appearance, brilliance, or delivery, or by rejecting the speaker because he is not like them: "He doesn't understand my problems"; "Maybe he can do it, but that's no sign we can"; "What does she know about children, she's never been a mother." Only infrequently, and as a result of great skill, does a speaker succeed in bridging the usual psychological distance between himself and his audience and move them to a point of social action.

When a speech is given at a large meeting, how can audience members participate actively? How can the presentation of a speech be arranged so that the speaker also learns and gains from the meeting? Although ingenuity undoubtedly can produce many more methods, the following illustrations are a sample of methods that bring increased participation, keener listening, greater involvement, and more lasting results:

■ A well-known speaker delivering a speech to over a hundred persons agrees to use some novel methods. Those attending are seated in movable chairs. Before introducing the speaker, the moderator makes a brief charge to the audience. He asks them to divide into quarters, according to where they are seated, and listen to the speech with a specific task in mind:

Quarter 1. Listen for questions the audience might like to ask the speaker.

Quarter 2. Recall experiences that would amplify or illustrate the theme of the speech.

Quarter 3. Note any disagreements with the points of view expressed by the speaker.

Quarter 4. Think of further points the speaker should make.

After the speech, the thirty or so members in each quarter are asked to swing their chairs around in small circles of six or eight to discuss their task. After fifteen minutes, the moderator samples the reactions of some of the groups in each section of the audience. The speaker thanks the group for their reactions and gives brief responses to questions.

Although the expanded meeting consumes an extra hour, the speaker reports that he has never had such an attentive audience nor has he received immediate and forthright reactions from an audience before, and the reactions are helpful to him. Members of the audience leave the meeting with both a feeling of having participated and a keener understanding of what the speaker said.

■ In another situation, a professor informs a large university class that, at the next class meeting, a visiting lecturer will talk to the class about a specific aspect of the subject they are studying. He is eager to base his talk on specific student interests and needs. The professor recommends that the students spend the present class hour working in small groups to compose a list of specific areas and items the lecturer might cover. He suggests that three or four volunteers record the groups' lists and combine them into a manageable list for the next meeting.

When the visiting lecturer arrives, he sees on the blackboard a series of questions and areas the class hopes he will deal with.

He tells the students he welcomes this help and then takes a moment or so to review the questions and establish a general background into which they can fit. Expressing the hope that his responses to the students' interests will raise even more questions, he suggests that rather than take notes, they jot down ideas and questions that occur to them. Then he allots part of his speech time for interaction between members of the class and himself.

By fitting his knowledge around student concerns and by actively involving them in planned dialogue, the lecturer makes his appearance a joint participative affair in which his "expert" status is reduced. He and the class members work as a team on a common area of interest.

■ A series of meetings on parent-child relationships is being held in the community with many parents attending. At the first two meetings, "experts" talk on the causes of difficult and delinquent child behavior. These talks are not very effective because they fail to fit the particular problems concerning most parents.

Consequently, the organizers plan to collect lists of parental concerns during the latter portion of the third meeting. They organize the parents into small discussion groups of six to eight. Each group has one member make a list of the problems expressed in that group. Discussion produces a considerable number of problems, but the lists from each group are very similar. At the end of this meeting, the organizers collect the lists and promise that the next meeting will deal with some of the concerns listed.

During the week between the third and fourth meeting, the organizers condense the lists into one list, find a resource person with a strong practical orientation, and persuade three parents who have regularly attended the meetings to take part in a role-playing activity.

When the parents arrive at the fourth meeting, they see the composite list printed on the blackboard, with one item, *discipline,* checked. Announcing that discipline is mentioned most frequently on the groups' lists, the leader suggests and describes a brief role play of two parents applying discipline. The scene they play is a situation of a twelve-year-old child, in trouble in school, who takes money from his mother's purse, and fails to tell the truth about his activities. Before starting the role-playing scene, the leader forms three observer teams:

1. Team One watches the parents, both in terms of their actions and their feelings, as the scene progresses.
2. Team Two watches the person playing the part of the child and evaluates the child's feelings as the parents endeavor to discipline him.
3. Team Three watches with the purpose of suggesting things the parents might have done.

With this introduction the three role players go through the scene. After about twenty minutes the meeting leader stops the scene and seeks reactions from members of the three observer teams. The response is exciting: the feelings of both parents and child are explored and the actions of those acting the part of the parents are analyzed and criticized.

With this background of active participation by all who attend the meeting, and with an actual scene to refer to, the resource person is able to be very helpful in talking about the difficult problem of understanding all the factors causing the child's behavior. The meeting is an outstanding success in the view of those attending.

CHAPTER  11

PLANNING THE
WORK-GROUP CONFERENCE

Most people want to participate in solving their own problems. The work conference provides an opportunity for groups of people to determine, consider, diagnose, and solve common problems. It has the value of training conference participants in the skills of working together as a group. A work conference more readily leads toward necessary action and change than the typical conference at which the participant sits passively listening to others think and decide for him.

Work conferences have been growing in popularity throughout the country. This is true not only for two- to four-week workshops but also for the one-, two-, or three-day conference. There are , however, a number of serious weaknesses in many work conferences. The major weakness, of course, lies in the fact that merely bringing people together to discuss does not necessarily ensure either answers or action. It may merely produce, as some have said, the pooling of ignorance. For many people,the opportunity to talk about a problem produces the illusion that the problem is solved. As a consequence, ordinary discussion-based conferences frequently leave people with a false feeling of accomplishment.

These weaknesses are very real and definitely must be guarded against, but they are not necessarily inherent in work conferences. They really demand more basic understanding of the principles necessary for successful work conferences. Research in work-conference methods has been undertaken in various parts of the country. It is on the basis of these research findings that we can look more analytically at conferences and plan them more successfully.

Attitudes and Principles

The work conference must rest on the following basic attitudes:

- The planners of work conferences should have implicit faith that people, with assistance in the process of developing group productivity, can reach a higher quality of thinking and decision making in groups than they can as individuals.

- "Telling" is not necessarily the best or the only way of inducing change in others.
- The important persons at a conference are the delegates. Leaders, resource persons, and consultants are servants to delegate groups. Obviously, this attitude is in opposition to those conferences that exalt the few.

These attitudes lead very definitely into certain principles underlying the designing of successful work conferences:

- The conference should focus on problems rather than general topics. The delegates need to acknowledge these problems as their own. The future of education is not a problem until it is approached from an angle such as "How may I continue to be a productive teacher under changing situations?"
- Participants should be involved both before and during the conference in making basic decisions. Only in this way will they feel that a conference belongs to them; it deals with their problems; and the conference planners do not decide what participants should think. The conference should be designed so that changes in its structure can be made whenever necessary.
- To assist delegate groups to think straight about their problems, every session of the conference should have an important and unique place in the total design and be planned in relation to the other sessions and their purposes.
- Periodically, delegates should be given the opportunity and assistance to evaluate both conference product and process in order that continuous improvement in both may be possible.
- There should be steady progress from problem selection to diagnosis; to solution decisions; to action.

Using the framework of these attitudes and principles, the planning of a work conference becomes more readily accomplished.

Planning Committee

It is customary for a committee to plan a conference. Its purpose is to make sure that the conference considers the needs and points of view of all the participants. Because there is no guarantee that the committee members are at all competent in the techniques of conference planning, they need either an outside consultant or one or more informed members of the committee to provide guidance. Their goal is a conference design that will most efficiently enable participants to organize themselves into groups, to find and diagnose their problems, and to arrive at problem solutions.

Participant Involvement

The success of a work conference can be measured by the degree to which the participants feel they have played a part in planning and implementing the conference, and whether they believe it is really dealing with their problems. There are many ways of involving members in a conference. An introductory letter can ask them if they feel a conference is called for at this time, and it can request a list of their crucial problems. These problems can be categorized into problem areas and sent back to allow the potential participants to select the area in which they wish to work.

Another way of involvement is to write to members concerning the type of conference to be held and the consequent responsibility they might assume. This is particularly important in conferences that depend upon complete delegate participation. Participants who come to a conference without having been involved cannot feel that the conference is their conference.

Changing Participant Expectancies

Because participants believe they are expected to remain passive and anonymous at a conference, they do not expect it to help them with their back-home problems. They need help to realize what they can accomplish in an efficient work conference. Otherwise, the shock of being expected to be active at a conference may set up patterns of aggression and block productivity. There are many ways of changing participants' expectancies. A printed program can give the conference agenda in one column, and in a parallel column show brief statements of what each session will require of the participants. The opening session of a work conference should give participants a picture of what the conference will be like.

Conference Design

In a well-planned conference there is no extra time for which something must be planned. There is no session when "This would be a good time to let Doctor So-and-So make a speech." Each part of the conference should follow a logical order and have a definite purpose in terms of the total conference design.

The following is a work-conference design that may be adapted for different purposes; there are, of course, many variations on this very general pattern:

1. An orientation session (or sessions) helps participants decide what results they want from the conference and what must be done by the staff and participants to achieve these results.
2. The conference groups meet and start selecting, discussing, and diagnosing their common problem.
3. A general session follows in which the conference groups report their progress and their problems to each other and stimulate more group work.
4. The work groups then continue working for one or two more sessions.
5. The conference meets as a whole again to determine how far it has gone and what its new problems are.
6. The groups meet and complete their work.
7. The conference comes together as a whole to examine its production and to make final decisions for action.

Conference Staff

Because there are specific conference functions that must be handled, they probably should be divided among the overall conference staff. Individual staff members can accept the following responsibilities:

1. Coordinating the conference
2. Training group leaders
3. Training group recorders and editing the daily and final progress reports
4. Training group observers, planning general sessions, and evaluating meetings
5. Managing the clerical staff and the physical facilities

No one person can efficiently handle all of these functions.

Orientation Sessions

The opening session of a conference has a major purpose: making it possible for participants and staff to reach basic agreements on the purpose and direction of the conference and the responsibilities of both participants and staff. All too frequently conference participants have one set of expectations for the conference, while the staff and leaders have another set. These different expectations typically cause confusion and frustration, blocking conference productivity.

Welcome speeches, a nice courtesy to incoming participants, are only an incidental part of an opening session. Too many conferences use welcome as the theme for the first meeting, thereby postponing productive conference discussion and thought.

An opening orientation session might well attempt to (a) describe the steps and stages of conference planning, indicating that all major decisions are yet to be made by participants, and those decisions made by staff were only planning services to aid participants rather than to direct them; (b) review with the participants the problems selected through pre-conference correspondence for consideration and solution; and (c) explore the problems of group productivity, the responsibilities to be accepted by members, and the service roles to be played by group leaders, recorders, observers, and resource persons. Frequently a spontaneous demonstration of how a group swings into production does much to help participants move immediately into good group discussion.

Selecting and Training Leaders

The group leader carries the basic role of the conference, although the key to a successful work conference is the service team for each group —a leader, an observer, and a recorder. Of course, a group leader must be informed in the area of discussion, but his main orientation should be toward helping the group develop its ability to discuss and solve problems. The person with a compulsion to solve problems for the group can be given a different conference role. High on the list of criteria for selection of leaders are sensitivity to the needs, progress, and goals of a group and skill in helping the members free their own potential abilities and resources for production.

No matter how skilled individuals are as group discussion leaders, experience shows that a pre-service training program measurably increases their effectiveness and the success of the conference. Such a training program usually is a half day to a day in length. First, it should orient leaders to (a) the design of the conference; (b) the type of participants expected; (c) the problem areas; (d) the roles of group observer and recorder; and (e) the assistance the leader can expect from the group observer and recorder and from other members of the staff.

A quick survey of areas in which the leaders expect the most difficulty reveals obvious needs for practice. Usually such areas are getting the group started, helping them keep on the track, and keeping the dominant members in check. Spontaneous practice sessions can then be carried on in these crucial areas. Final practice can be given in ways in which the leader and observer work together in an evaluation session, and in ways in which leader, recorder, and observer can form a closely knit service team for the group.

Selecting and Training Recorders

The group recorder helps the group keep track of its production. When the group needs a check on where it is or where it has gone, or when it needs to summarize progress, the recorder is its resource. Furthermore, each participant wants to be kept informed of what is happening in other groups. The group recorders, working with one staff member, can prepare a succinct daily summary of conference progress which can be duplicated in the form of a daily newspaper and given to each participant or presented at a general session as a news broadcast "from us to us." Finally, the recorders have major responsibility for preparing the final conference report.

General Sessions

General sessions, the times when the conference as a whole comes together, play a specific and important part in a work conference. These sessions determine whether the conference remains a collection of subgroups or is welded together into a cohesive large group. General sessions may have a variety of other purposes. They may be used as opportunities for the conference to consider its progress, to evaluate how it is working, and to consider new problems that have arisen during the conference period. General sessions should always be flexible enough to permit changes to meet sudden conference needs.

Information Sessions

Information sessions are sessions in which information needed by subgroups for further consideration of their problems is given in the most efficient manner. It may be a succinct and fact-crammed talk, a film, a dialogue, or a panel, depending upon the information needed and the resources at hand. Information sessions differ in many ways from typical speeches. They make no effort to convince, to argue, or to beguile. They are essentially sessions scheduled after the conference groups recognize the need for certain information.

Resource Persons

Every conference needs resource persons—individuals who have specific information, experiences, skills, or points of view useful to the group. However, the use of such resource persons demands planning and skill. Unless the group knows how to use the resource person in terms of its needs and unless the resource person knows how to contribute wisely, he may dominate the group, lead it away from its goal, or fail to contribute needed information. Few conferences successfully use resource persons.

Final Session

Each conference should evaluate the various group products, make necessary total conference decisions, and plan ways of implementing these decisions in action. The final session may well become a commitment session in which organizations, groups, and individuals publicly commit themselves to future action. Research indicates that such commitments are one of the strong forces for inducing change. In any event, the final session should help participants realize the progress made by the conference and think through the further demands of this progress.

CHAPTER

CONCLUSION

An individual who creates the solutions to his problems and makes his own decisions develops pride and a sense of ownership in their implementation. Success in making and implementing decisions also increases an individual's willingness and ability to tackle even more difficult problems.

Most individuals need to belong to a small group that means something to them, and they seek acceptance from its members. Then as they play a more meaningful role in that group, their sense of belonging increases.

A group possesses an identity, an atmosphere, a behavior pattern of its own. A collection of individuals can become a productive group—a group that grows in its ability to handle both its tasks and its internal maintenance problems.

These realizations—the human need to be involved in a group and the impact of an individual's behavior on the competency of the group—lead to a concept of group leadership very different from the traditional viewpoint.

These points and others have provided major themes for this book, and my thesis, based on these themes, is a simple one: meetings work when leadership is conceived as service given to group members as they perform their task.

Leadership as service commits the leader to helping the group, and to meeting the individual's needs to belong and to be involved. Leadership as service stresses helping group members to understand and cope with interpersonal, power, and methodological problems that are internal to group operation. Leadership as service means sharing leadership functions with group members and helping them learn not only those functions related to the problem to be solved or the decision to be made, but a variety of group-oriented roles.

Without further professional training, but with this view of leadership and group behavior, leaders can learn to observe how a group works as well as what it accomplishes. As leaders observe groups on both levels—task performance and group maintenance and growth—they can recognize many of the important aspects of group behavior. With their help, group members can all recognize these aspects and join with the leader in coping with group problems.

Making meetings work requires a leader who is willing to risk being creative, imaginative, and effective, a leader who invites and challenges group members to take the same risks. Meetings work because people learn to trust and cooperate as they work together.

SELECTED BIBLIOGRAPHY

Argyris, C. *Management and organization development.* New York: McGraw-Hill, 1971.

Beckhard, R. *Strategies of organization development.* Reading, Mass.: Addison-Wesley, 1969.

Benne, K. D., & Bradford, L. P. The annual conference of the department of adult education. *Adult Education Bulletin,* December 1948, *13*(2).

Benne, K. D., & Muntyan, B. *Human relations and curriculum change.* New York: Dryden, 1951.

Benne, K. D., & Sheats, P. Functional roles of group members. *Journal of Social Issues,* Spring 1948, *4*(2).

Bradford, L. P. Planning the work group conference. *Adult Education Bulletin,* February 1948, *12*(3).

Bradford, L. P. Leading the large meeting. *Adult Education Bulletin,* December 1949, *14*(2).

Bradford, L. P. A fundamental of democracy. *Adult Education Bulletin,* April 1952, *2*(4).

Bradford, L. P. The case of the hidden agenda. *Adult Leadership,* September 1952, *1*(4).

Bradford, L. P. The class as a group. *The High School Journal,* 1961, *44*(8).

Bradford, L. P. (Ed.). *Group development.* Arlington, Va.: NTL Institute for Applied Behavioral Science, 1961. Reissued: La Jolla, Calif.: University Associates, 1976.

Bradford, L. P., & Corey, S. M. Improving large group meetings. *Adult Education Bulletin,* April 1951, *16*(4).

Bradford, L. P., & Lippitt, R. Building a democratic work group. *Personnel,* 1945, *22*(3).

Bradford, L. P., & Sheats, P. Complacency shock as a prerequisite to training. *Societry,* 1948, *2*(1).

Bradford, L. P., Stock, D., & Horwitz, M. How to diagnose group problems. *Adult Leadership,* December 1953, *2*(7).

Burke, W. W., & Beckhard, R. (Eds.). *Conference planning* (2nd ed.). Arlington, Va.: NTL Institute for Applied Behavioral Science, 1962. Reissued: La Jolla, Calif.: University Associates, 1976.

Kaufman, R. *Identifying and solving problems: A system approach.* La Jolla, Calif.: University Associates, 1976.

Knowles, M., & Knowles, H. *How to develop better leaders.* New York: Association Press, 1955.

Lassey, W. R., & Fernández, R. R. (Eds.). *Leadership and social change* (2nd ed.). La Jolla, Calif.: University Associates, 1976.

Lippitt, G. L. (Ed.). *Leadership in action.* Arlington, Va.: NTL Institute for Applied Behavioral Science, 1961.

Lippitt, R., Bradford, L. P. , & Benne, K. D. Sociodramatic clarification of leader and group roles as a starting point for effective group functioning. *Society,* 1946, *1*(1).

Marrow, A., Bowers, D. G., & Seashore, S. E. *Management by participation.* New York: Harper & Row, 1967.

McGregor, D. *The human side of enterprise.* New York: McGraw-Hill, 1960.

Schindler-Rainman, E., & Lippitt, R. *Taking your meetings out of the doldrums.* Columbus, Ohio: Association of Professional Directors, 1975.

Strauss, B., & Strauss, F. *New ways to better meetings.* New York: The Viking Press, 1951.

White, R. K., & Lippitt, R. *Autocracy and democracy.* New York: Harper & Row, 1960.

APPENDIXES
INTRODUCTION

Developing a participative, creative, and productive group requires a leader who is concerned with the maintenance and building of the group, as well as with its task performance. And task performance can be more easily secured by attention to maintenance and building. The development of an effective group calls for a definite philosophy of leadership, sensitivity to group process, and specific methods and skills.

WAYS OF BUILDING AN EFFECTIVE GROUP

Given the tradition that the leader is responsible for all aspects of a group's process and product, group members tend to lack responsibility. It is up to the leader of such a group to encourage and assist members in sharing the functions that are necessary for effective decision making and the members' full participation and satisfaction with the group.

The leader's efforts to share leadership responsibility can include:

- making a verbal contract with the group;
- modeling appropriate examples of maintaining and developing the group;
- suggesting action or reporting information when no one else offers it.

THE LEADER'S CONTRACT

At the beginning of the meeting, the leader should explain his contract with the group, for example:

> I hope we can all feel equal ownership in the group—it is *our* group, not *my* group. Each of us can feel responsible and free to help the group be productive, involving, and satisfying. I do not intend to direct the group, but to serve it—in any way I can. Decisions should be made by group members and not solely by me. I guess this gives each of you the responsibility for keeping on the beam, while not rejecting important contributions from anyone; for encouraging free and open participation; for recognizing and solving problems that are distracting the group; and for helping each other to develop member-leader skills. I promise to be as helpful as I can.

SECURING INFORMATION FROM BEHAVIOR

Behavioral evidence that a group is getting into difficulties often goes unrecognized, is ignored, or is deliberately not brought out into the open. Ways of bringing such behavior into the group's discussion can be modeled by the leader in a manner that places no blame or punishment. This demonstration by the leader trains the members and enables them to perform the same function later. For example:

> I've noticed that during the last half hour more and more members have withdrawn from the discussion, leaving only two or three members actively participating. Have any of you also observed this? What does it mean? Will it affect our progress on the task? How are the silent members feeling?

or:

> Not long ago almost everyone was leaning forward, apparently very involved in the discussion. Lately more and more members are slumped back in their chairs. Has this become obvious? What does it mean for our work as a group?

SECURING INFORMATION FROM FEELINGS AND PERCEPTIONS

Sometimes an individual's feelings and perceptions, with or without behavioral data, can serve as indicators of poor group process. Again, in early meetings, the leader can model how to bring such feelings to the surface and check on whether they are shared by others:

> For the last twenty minutes, I've sensed considerable tension in the group. Looking around, I see faces that look a little more tense or more flushed, and the noise level seems to have risen. Has anyone else felt this way? What is happening in the group?

DIAGNOSING

Once there is some agreement in the group that there is a problem, the next step is diagnosing the cause of the difficulty. There are a number of ways in which a leader can suggest a method of diagnosis. Philip Hanson's "What to Look for in Groups" (Appendix A) can serve as an observation guide for the leader and group members.

If the problem is not too difficult for the group to face openly, the leader can suggest a discussion that seeks to uncover the problem. If the problem is related to the task, rather than to feeling or interpersonal causes, an immediate discussion may be sufficient. If sufficient experience and trust has been developed in the group, open discussion may still be possible, such as the following expression from a member:

> I feel that we are polarizing the issue, with the result that no one is really hearing anyone else. We are arguing and some people have withdrawn rather than become involved in the argument.

Another method that can serve as a preliminary to a diagnostic discussion is anonymous diagnoses. Each person, including the leader, writes a diagnosis of the problem on a slip of paper, folds the paper, and places it in the middle of the table. The papers are scrambled and one member reads them aloud. When numerous diagnoses are voiced, they lead to further discussion.

SOLUTION SEEKING

Leaders and members need to acquire sensitive timing in the use of specific task functions. If sufficient information is not sought or ideas are not listened to, an inadequate decision can result. On the other hand, seeking more information than is necessary can slow decision making or create a group fear of coming to a decision. A summary made too early, or a vote called for too rapidly, can cut off contributions that could be vital to an effective decision. On the other hand, delaying a summary may leave members with confused ideas about what has transpired, or the delay may be used as a manipulative tool by a subgroup to win an argument.

An effective leader who is sensitive to the appropriate timing for specific task solving functions tries by encouragement and modeling to develop the same skills in group members.

THE USE OF FEEDBACK

The member whose behavior is dysfunctional to the group needs to become aware of the consequences of that behavior on the group, on individual members, and on the task solution. If the member exhibiting the dysfunctional behavior fails to learn what is disruptive about the behavior, it may occur time after time.

Feedback from other group members, as Appendix B describes in detail, is a basic way of eliminating dysfunctional behavior from an individual or a subgroup. Feedback is reporting, without assigning blame, the impact of an individual's behavior on others; usually with the assumption that the individual is not aware of that impact. Feedback should be given in a caring manner with the purpose of helping the individual and the group.

Appendix B discusses the difficulty of giving feedback properly, the need for a group atmosphere of trust and caring, and the problem of handling natural defensiveness.

A leader can slowly and carefully demonstrate effective methods of giving feedback. As feedback is successfully used and accepted as helpful, trust among members increases.

MEETING EVALUATION FORMS

Appendixes C, D, E, F, G, and H are examples of brief evaluation forms that are useful for recording participant reaction shortly before the end of the meeting. This data can be used in a number of ways:

- The forms are collected and a summary of the results is announced at the next meeting.
- After completing the form, participants are clustered in small groups to discuss their evaluation. Each subgroup presents a brief summary.
- The group leader selects themes from several forms and asks for evaluation only on those themes.
- The evaluation form is used by only one member, who serves as a participant-observer for the meeting. This role may be rotated so that all participants have an opportunity.
- The group collects observations on several meetings and then devotes an entire session to looking at the maintenance issues reflected in the evaluation forms.

These forms are included here to illustrate ways in which more formal evaluation data can be collected. The group will undoubtedly think of other uses for these or similar evaluation forms. A word of caution: it is possible to overdo written evaluations and to develop a "we must be perfect" climate. Often is it more useful, especially for a small group, to ask participants for a verbal evaluation in the final fifteen minutes of the meetings.

USE OF THE APPENDIXES

Group leaders may want to assign these readings as "homework" for members or lead a short discussion in each meeting session on one of the topics suggested by the forms.

These appendixes may be duplicated without special permission from the publisher for free distribution to meeting members.

Appendix A
WHAT TO LOOK FOR IN GROUPS
Philip G. Hanson

In all human interactions there are two major ingredients — content and process. The first deals with the subject matter or the task upon which the group is working. In most interactions, the focus of attention of all persons is on the content. The second ingredient, process, is concerned with what is happening between and to group members while the group is working. Group process, or dynamics, deals with such items as morale, feeling tone, atmosphere, influence, participation, styles of influence, leadership struggles, conflict, competition, cooperation, etc. In most interactions, very little attention is paid to process, even when it is the major cause of ineffective group action. Sensitivity to group process will better enable one to diagnose group problems early and deal with them more effectively. Since these processes are present in all groups, awareness of them will enhance a person's worth to a group and enable him to be a more effective group participant.

Below are some observation guidelines to help one process analyze group behavior.

Participation

One indication of involvement is verbal participation. Look for differences in the amount of participation among members.

1. Who are the high participators?
2. Who are the low participators?
3. Do you see any shift in participation, e.g., highs become quiet; lows suddenly become talkative. Do you see any possible reason for this in the group's interaction?
4. How are the silent people treated? How is their silence interpreted? Consent? Disagreement? Disinterest? Fear? etc.
5. Who talks to whom? Do you see any reason for this in the group's interactions?
6. Who keeps the ball rolling? Why? Do you see any reason for this in the group's interactions?

Influence

Influence and participation are not the same. Some people may speak very little, yet they capture the attention of the whole group. Others may talk a lot but are generally not listened to by other members.

7. Which members are high in influence? That is, when they talk others seem to listen.
8. Which members are low in influence? Others do not listen to or follow them. Is there any shifting in influence? Who shifts?
9. Do you see any rivalry in the group? Is there a struggle for leadership? What effect does it have on other group members?

Reprinted from J. William Pfeiffer and John E. Jones (Eds.), *The 1972 Annual Handbook for Group Facilitators*, La Jolla, Calif.: University Associates, 1972. Used with permission of the publisher.

Styles of Influence

Influence can take many forms. It can be positive or negative; it can enlist the support or cooperation of others or alienate them. *How* a person attempts to influence another may be the crucial factor in determining how open or closed the other will be toward being influenced. Items 10 through 13 are suggestive of four styles that frequently emerge in groups.

10. Autocratic: Does anyone attempt to impose his will or values on other group members or try to push them to support his decisions? Who evaluates or passes judgment on other group members? Do any members block action when it is not moving the direction they desire? Who pushes to "get the group organized"?

11. Peacemaker: Who eagerly supports other group members' decisions? Does anyone consistently try to avoid conflict or unpleasant feelings from being expressed by pouring oil on the troubled waters? Is any member typically deferential toward other group members — gives them power? Do any members appear to avoid giving negative feedback, *i.e.*, who will level only when they have positive feedback to give?

12. Laissez faire: Are any group members getting attention by their apparent lack of involvement in the group? Does any group member go along with group decisions without seeming to commit himself one way or the other? Who seems to be withdrawn and uninvolved; who does not initiate activity, participates mechanically and only in response to another member's question?

13. Democratic: Does anyone try to include everyone in a group decision or discussion? Who expresses his feelings and opinions openly and directly without evaluating or judging others? Who appears to be open to feedback and criticisms from others? When feelings run high and tension mounts, which members attempt to deal with the conflict in a problem-solving way?

Decision-Making Procedures

Many kinds of decisions are made in groups without considering the effects of these decisions on other members. Some people try to impose their own decisions on the group, while others want all members to participate or share in the decisions that are made.

14. Does anyone make a decision and carry it out without checking with other group members? (Self-authorized) For example, he decides on the topic to be discussed and immediately begins to talk about it. What effect does this have on other group members?

15. Does the group drift from topic to topic? Who topic-jumps? Do you see any reason for this in the group's interactions?

16. Who supports other members' suggestions or decisions? Does this support result in the two members deciding the topic or activity for the group (handclasp)? How does this effect other group members?

17. Is there any evidence of a majority pushing a decision through over other members objections? Do they call for a vote (majority support)?

18. Is there any attempt to get all members participating in a decision (consensus)? What effect does this seem to have on the group?

19. Does anyone make any contributions which do not receive any kind of response or recognition (plop)? What effect does this have on the member?

Task Functions

These functions illustrate behaviors that are concerned with getting the job done, or accomplishing the task that the group has before them.

20. Does anyone ask for or make suggestions as to the best way to proceed or to tackle a problem?
21. Does anyone attempt to summarize what has been covered or what has been going on in the group?
22. Is there any giving or asking for facts, ideas, opinions, feelings, feedback, or searching for alternatives?
23. Who keeps the group on target? Who prevents topic-jumping or going off on tangents?

Maintenance Functions

These functions are important to the morale of the group. They maintain good and harmonious working relationships among the members and create a group atmosphere which enables each member to contribute maximally. They insure smooth and effective teamwork within the group.

24. Who helps others get into the discussion (gate openers)?
25. Who cuts off others or interrupts them (gate closers)?
26. How well are members getting their ideas across? Are some members preoccupied and not listening? Are there any attempts by group members to help others clarify their ideas?
27. How are ideas rejected? How do members react when their ideas are not accepted? Do members attempt to support others when they reject their ideas?

Group Atmosphere

Something about the way a group works creates an atmosphere which in turn is revealed in a general impression. In addition, people may differ in the kind of atmosphere they like in a group. Insight can be gained into the atmosphere characteristic of a group by finding words which describe the general impressions held by group members.

28. Who seems to prefer a friendly congenial atmosphere? Is there any attempt to suppress conflict or unpleasant feelings?
29. Who seems to prefer an atmosphere of conflict and disagreement? Do any members provoke or annoy others?
30. Do people seem involved and interested? Is the atmosphere one of work, play satisfaction, taking flight, sluggishness, etc.?

Membership

A major concern for group members is the degree of acceptance or inclusion in the group. Different patterns of interaction may develop in the group which give clues to the degree and kind of membership.

31. Is there any sub-grouping? Some times two or three members may consistently agree and support each other or consistently disagree and oppose one another.
32. Do some people seem to be "outside" the group? Do some members seem to be "in"? How are those "outside" treated?

33. Do some members move in and out of the group, *e.g.*, lean forward or backward in their chairs or move their chairs in and out? Under what conditions do they come in or move out?

Feelings

During any group discussion, feelings are frequently generated by the interactions between members. These feelings, however, are seldom talked about. Observers may have to make guesses based on tone of voice, facial expressions, gestures, and many other forms of nonverbal cues.

34. What signs of feelings do you observe in group members: anger, irritation, frustration, warmth, affection, excitement, boredom, defensiveness, competitiveness, etc.?

35. Do you see any attempts by group members to block the expression of feelings, particularly negative feelings? How is this done? Does anyone do this consistently?

Norms

Standards or ground rules may develop in a group that control the behavior of its members. Norms usually express the beliefs or desires of the majority of the group members as to what behaviors *should* or *should not* take place in the group. These norms may be clear to all members (explicit), known or sensed by only a few (implicit), or operating completely below the level of awareness of any group members. Some norms facilitate group progress and some hinder it.

36. Are certain areas avoided in the group (*e.g.*, sex, religion, talk about present feelings in group, discussing the leader's behavior, etc.)? Who seems to reinforce this avoidance? How do they do it?

37. Are group members overly nice or polite to each other? Are only positive feelings expressed? Do members agree with each other too readily? What happens when members disagree?

38. Do you see norms operating about participation or the kinds of questions that are allowed (*e.g.*, "If I talk, you must talk"; "If I tell my problems you have to tell your problems")? Do members feel free to probe each other about their feelings? Do questions tend to be restricted to intellectual topics or events outside of the group?

Appendix B
GIVING FEEDBACK: AN INTERPERSONAL SKILL
Philip G. Hanson

The process of giving and asking for feedback is probably the most important dimension of laboratory education. It is through feedback that we can learn to "see ourselves as others see us." This, of course, is not an easy task. Effectively giving and receiving feedback implies certain key ingredients: caring, trusting, acceptance, openness, and a concern for the needs of others. Thus, how evaluative, judgmental, or helpful feedback is may finally depend on the personal philosophy of the individuals involved. Nevertheless, giving feedback is a *skill* that can be learned and developed and for which certain useful guidelines exist.

The term "feedback" was borrowed from rocket engineering by Kurt Lewin, a founder of laboratory education. A rocket sent into space contains a mechanism that sends signals back to Earth. On Earth, a steering apparatus receives these signals, makes adjustments if the rocket is off target, and corrects its course. The group can be seen as such a steering mechanism, sending signals when group members are off target in terms of the goals they have set for themselves. These signals—feedback—can then be used by an individual to correct his course. For example, a person's goal may be to become more aware of himself and to learn how his behavior affects others. Information from the group can help him to ascertain whether he is moving toward this goal. If he reacts to criticisms of his behavior by getting angry, leaving the room, or otherwise acting defensively, he will not reach his goal. Group members may help him by saying, "George, every time we give you feedback, you do something that keeps us from giving you further information. If you continue this kind of behavior, you will not reach your goal." If George responds to the "steering" of the group by adjusting his direction, he can again move toward his target. Feedback, then, is a technique that helps members of a group achieve their goals. It is also a means of comparing one's own perceptions of his behavior with others' perceptions.

Giving feedback is a verbal or nonverbal process through which an individual lets others know his perceptions and feelings about *their* behavior. When *soliciting* feedback, an individual is asking for others' perceptions and feelings about *his* behavior. Most people give and receive feedback daily without being aware of doing so. One purpose of laboratory training is to increase the awareness of this process so that it can be engaged in intentionally rather than unconsciously.

INFORMATION-EXCHANGE PROCESS

Between two people, the process of exchange goes something like this: Person A's *intention* is to act in relation to person B, who sees only person A's *behavior*. Between his intention and his behavior comes an encoding process that person A uses to make his behavior congruent with his intentions. Person B perceives person A's behavior, interprets it (a decoding process), and intends to respond. Between person B's intention and his responding behavior an encoding process also occurs. Person A then perceives person B's responding behavior and interprets it. However, if either person's process is ineffective, the receiver may respond in a manner that will confuse the sender. Although the feedback process can help an individual discover whether his behavior is congruent with his intentions, the process focuses on *behavior* rather than on *intentions*. An individual's intentions are private; unless he explains them, other people can only conjecture

Reprinted from John E. Jones and J. William Pfeiffer (Eds.), *The 1975 Annual Handbook for Group Facilitators*, La Jolla, Calif.: University Associates, 1975. Used with permission of the publisher.

what those intentions are. One of the most confusing aspects of communication is that people tend to give feedback about other people's *intentions,* rather than their *behavior.* Causing further confusion is the fact that many people perceive behavior as being negatively intended, when in fact it is not. It is often difficult to see that the sender's intentions may not be what they are perceived to be.

RESPONSIBILITY FOR FEEDBACK

In many feedback exchanges, the question of ownership frequently arises: How much responsibility should the giver assume for his behavior and the receiver for his response? If person A behaves so that he evokes a negative response (feedback) from person B, how much ownership should each assume for his part of the interaction? Some people are willing to assume more than their share of the responsibility for another person's responses, while others refuse to own any responsibility for their behavior.

For example, an individual may be habitually late for group meetings and may receive feedback concerning members' negative reactions to this behavior. His response is to point out to the group members their lack of tolerance for individual differences. He says that they are limiting his freedom and that they seem to be investing too much responsibility in him for the group's effectiveness. He states that he wants to be involved in the group, but he does not understand why they need him to be on time.

This situation presents a value dilemma to the group; his observations are accurate, but his behavior is provocative. One clarification of this dilemma is to point out that, while an individual owns only his behavior, the reactions of others inevitably affect him. To the extent that he cares about the others or his relationship with them, he must consider their responses.

Concern for the needs of others as well as one's own is a critical dimension in the exchange of feedback. Ownership or responsibility for one's behavior and the consequences of that behavior overlap between the giver and receiver of feedback. The problem lies in reaching some mutual agreement concerning where one person's responsibility ends and the other's begins.

GUIDELINES FOR USING FEEDBACK

It is possible to minimize a person's defensiveness in receiving feedback and to maximize his ability to use it for his personal growth. Regardless of how accurate feedback may be, if a person cannot accept the information because he is defensive, then feedback is useless. Feedback must be given so that the person receiving it can *hear* it in the most objective and least distorted way possible, *understand* it, and choose to *use* it or *not use* it.

The following guidelines are listed as if they were bipolar, with the second term in each dimension describing the more effective method of giving feedback. For example, in one group George, intending to compliment Marie, says to her, "I wish I could be more selfish, like you." Marie might respond, "Why, you insensitive boor, what do you mean by saying I'm selfish?" George might then get defensive and retaliate, and both people would become involved in the game of "who-can-hurt-whom-the-most." Instead, Marie might give George feedback by stating her position in another way. That is, she could say, "When you said, 'I wish I could be more selfish, like you,' I felt angry and degraded." This second method of giving feedback contains positive elements that the first does not.

Indirect vs. Direct Expression of Feelings

When Marie stated that George was an insensitive boor, she was expressing her feelings indirectly. That statement might imply that she was feeling angry or irritated, but one could not be certain. On the other hand, Marie expressed her feelings directly when she said, "I felt angry and degraded." She committed herself, and there was no need to guess her feelings. If Tom says to Andy, "I like you," he is expressing his feelings directly, risking rejection. However, if he says, "You are a likeable person," the risk is less. Indirect expression of feelings is safer because it is ambiguous. Andy might guess that Tom likes him, but Tom can always deny it. If Andy rejects Tom by saying, "I am happy to hear that I am likeable, but I do not like you," Tom can counter, "You are a likeable person, but *I* do not like you." Indirect expression of feelings offers an escape from commitment.

"You are driving too fast" is an indirect expression of feelings. "I am anxious because you are driving too fast" is a direct expression of feelings. Indirect statements often begin with "I feel that . . ." and finish with a perception or opinion, for example, "I feel that you are angry." This is an indirect expression or perception and does not state what "I" is feeling. Instead, "I am anxious because you look angry" expresses the speaker's feelings directly and also states a perception. People frequently assume that they are expressing their feelings directly when they state opinions and perceptions starting with "I feel that . . . ," but they are not.

Interpretation vs. Description of Behavior

In the original example in which Marie said to George, "When you said, 'I wish I could be more selfish, like you,' I felt angry and degraded," Marie was describing the behavior to which she was reacting. She was not attributing a motive to George's behavior, such as "You are hostile," or "You do not like me." When one attributes a motive to a person's behavior one is interpreting that person's *intention*. Since his intention is private and available only to him, interpretation of his behavior is highly questionable. In addition, one person's interpretations probably arise from a theory of personality that may not be shared by the other person. For example, if William is fidgeting in his chair and shuffling his feet, and Walter says, "You are anxious," Walter is interpreting William's behavior. Walter's theory of personality states that when a person fidgets in his chair and shuffles his feet, he is manifesting anxiety. Such a theory interposed between two people may create a distance between them or act as a barrier to understanding. If, instead, Walter *describes* William's behavior, William may interpret his own behavior by saying, "I need to go to the bathroom."

In any event, interpreting another person's behavior or ascribing motives to it tends to put that person on the defensive and makes him spend his energies on either explaining his behavior or defending himself. It deprives him of the opportunity to interpret or make sense of his own behavior and, at the same time, makes him dependent on the interpreter. The feedback, regardless of how much insight it contains, cannot be used.

Evaluative vs. Nonevaluative Feedback

Effective feedback to George was not accomplished by calling him names such as "insensitive boor" or, in other words, evaluating him as a person. When giving feedback, one must respond not to the personal worth of the person but to his *behavior*. When someone is told that he is "stupid" or "insensitive," it is extremely difficult for him to respond objectively. He may sometimes *act* stupidly or *behave* in an insensitive way, but that does not mean that he is a stupid or insensitive person. Evaluating a person casts one in the role of a judge and places that person in the role of being judged. In addition, a frame of reference or set of values is imposed that may not be applicable to, or shared by, other people. That is, the person making the evaluation assumes that he can distinguish between a "good" person and a "bad" person or between "right" and "wrong," and that if the receiver of the feedback does not exemplify these values, the sender will be unhappy with him.

Response to Evaluative Feedback

It is difficult for anyone to respond to evaluative feedback because it usually offends his feelings of worth and self-esteem. These are core concepts about ourselves that cannot be changed readily by feedback, nor can they be easily interpreted in terms of actual behavior. It is difficult, for example, to point out to an individual the specific behaviors that manifest low self-esteem. If a person is given feedback that he is "stupid," he may not know what *behaviors* to change. It is the person's observable behavior and not his self-esteem that must be responded to when giving feedback.

An additional problem with evaluative feedback is that it often engenders defensiveness. When this occurs, the feedback is not likely to be useful.

General vs. Specific Feedback

When Marie responded to George by saying, "When you said, 'I wish I could be more selfish, like you,' I felt angry and degraded," she was describing a *specific* behavior. If she had said, "You are hostile," she would have been giving feedback in *general* terms; George might not have known to which behavior she was reacting. The term "hostile" does not specify *what* evoked a response in Marie. If George wanted to change he would not know what behavior to change. However, when the sender is specific, the receiver knows to what behavior the sender is responding, which he can then change or modify. Feedback expressed in general terms, such as "You are a warm person," does not allow the receiver to know what specific behavior is perceived as warm. He cannot expand or build on this feedback until he knows which behavior evoked the response "warm."

Pressure to Change vs. Freedom of Choice to Change

When Marie told George that she felt angry and degraded by George's statement, she did not tell him he had to change his behavior. If she or the feedback were important to George, however, he would probably change anyway; if these were not important to him, he might decide not to change. A person should have the freedom to use feedback in any meaningful way without being required to change. When the giver of feedback tells a person to change, he is assuming that he knows the correct standards for right and wrong or good and bad behavior and that the receiver needs to adopt those standards for his own good (or to save the sender the trouble of changing). Imposing standards on another person and expecting him to conform arouses resistance and resentment. The sender assumes that his standards are superior. A major problem in marriages arises when spouses tell each other that they must change their behaviors and attitudes to conform with one or the other partner's expectations and demands. These pressures to change can be very direct or very subtle, creating a competitive, win-lose relationship.

Expression of Disappointment as Feedback

Sometimes feedback reflects the sender's disappointment that the receiver did not meet his expectations and hopes. For example, a group leader may be disappointed that a member did not actualize his potential impact on the group, or a professor may be disappointed in a student's lack of achievement. These situations represent a dilemma. An important part of the sender's feedback is his own feelings, whether they are disappointment or satisfaction; if he withholds these feelings and/or perceptions, he may give the receiver a false impression. If, however, he expresses his disappointment, the receiver may experience this feedback as an indication of personal failure instead of as an incentive to change.

Persistent Behavior

Frequently the complaint is heard that a group member persists in a behavior that others find irritating, despite the feedback he receives. Group members exclaim, "What are we supposed to do? He won't change!" The most the members can do is to continue to confront the offender with their feelings. While he has the freedom not to change, he will also have to accept the consequences of his decision, i.e., other people's continuing irritation at his behavior and their probable punitive reactions. He cannot reasonably expect other group members both to feel positive toward him and to accept the behavior they find irritating. The only person an individual can change is himself. As a by-product of his change, other people may change in relationship to him. As the individual changes, others will have to adjust their behavior to his. No one should be forced to change. Such pressure may produce superficial conformity, but also underlying resentment and anger.

Delayed vs. Immediate Timing

To be most effective, feedback should, whenever possible, be given immediately after the event. In the initial example of the exchange between George and Marie, if Marie had waited until the next day to give feedback, George might have responded with "I don't remember saying that," or if Marie had asked the other group members later they might have responded with only a vague recollection; the event had not been significant to them, although it had been to Marie.

When feedback is given immediately after the event, the event is fresh in everyone's mind. It is like a mirror of the person's behavior, reflected to him through feedback. Other group members can also contribute their observations about the interaction. There is often, however, a tendency to delay feedback. A person may fear losing control of his feelings, fear hurting the other person's feelings, or fear exposing himself to other people's criticisms. Nevertheless, although the "here-and-now" transactions of group life can often be most threatening, they can also be most exciting and growth producing.

Planned Feedback

An exception to this guideline is the periodic feedback session, planned to keep communication channels open. Staff members in work units or departments may have weekly feedback meetings, or a specific time may be set aside for structured or unstructured feedback sessions in one- or two-week workshops. In these scheduled sessions, participants may cover events occurring since the last session or may work with material generated during their current meeting. For this process to be effective, however, the decision to have these feedback sessions should be reached through a consensus of the participants.

External vs. Group-Shared Feedback

When feedback is given immediately after the event, it is usually group shared, so that other members can look at the interaction as it occurs. For example, if group members had reacted to George's statement ("I wish I could be more selfish, like you") by saying, "If I were in your shoes, Marie, I wouldn't have felt degraded" or "I did not perceive it as degrading," then Marie would have had to look at her behavior and its appropriateness. If, on the other hand, group members had supported Marie's feelings and perceptions (consensual validation), her feedback would have had more potency.

Events that occur outside the group ("there-and-then") may be known to only one or two group members and, consequently, cannot be reacted to or discussed meaningfully by other participants. In addition, other group members may

feel left out during these discussions. For example, when a group member is discussing an argument he had with his wife, the most assistance group members can provide is to attempt to perceive from his behavior in the group what occurred in that interaction and to share these conjectures with him. Since, in describing the event, the group member's perception is colored by his own bias and emotional involvement, group members may receive a distorted picture of the argument and may not be able to discriminate between fact and fiction. If the argument had occurred in the group, however, group members could have been helpful since they would have shared the event. Then, if the involved group member had begun describing his perceptions of what happened, other group members could have commented on or shared their perceptions of the interaction.

Use of There-and-Then

In other words, events within the group can be processed by all group members who witness the interaction; they can share their perceptions and feelings about what occurred. This does not mean that group members cannot get *some* value from describing events external to the group and receiving comments from other members. What happens frequently, however, is that the group member describes these events in such a way as to elicit support or confirmation of his own perceptions rather than objective evaluation. Yet this relation of there-and-then events to the here-and-now can often be extremely productive as back-home "bridges." It can also be productive when some members have had long-term relationships with one another. It is important, at these times, to recognize both the necessity and the difficulty of involving other group members in the discussion.

Consistent Perceptions

Shared perceptions of what happens in here-and-now events is one of the primary values of a group. "Group shared" also implies that, ideally, each member has to participate. Frequently a person gets feedback from *one* member in the group and assumes that the rest of the group feels the same. This is not always a correct assumption. Feedback from only one person may present a very private or distorted picture because that person's perceptions of the event may differ from other group members'. When everyone's reactions are given, however, the receiver has a much better view of his behavior. If the group members are consistent in their perception of the receiver, and this disagrees with the receiver's view of himself, then he needs to look more closely at the validity of his self-perceptions. Frequently the fact that people perceive an individual's behavior differently is useful information in itself. Part of each group member's responsibility is to ask for feedback from members who are not responding so that the receiver will know how everyone sees his behavior. The receiver may have to be somewhat aggressive and persistent in seeking this information. Group members may tend to say "me, too" when their feedback is being given by someone else. When *all* the data have been obtained, the receiver is in a better position to make a more effective decision regarding his use of the feedback.

Imposed vs. Solicited Feedback

In most exchanges, feedback is usually imposed. People give feedback whether it is solicited or not and whether the person is prepared to receive it or not. In addition, the sender's need to give feedback may be much greater than the individual's need to receive it. This is particularly true when the sender is upset about something concerning the potential recipient. In many situations, it is legitimate to impose feedback, particularly when a norm exists for giving as well as for soliciting feedback, or in order to induce a norm of spontaneity. However, feedback is usually more helpful when the person solicits it. Asking for feedback may indicate that the receiver is prepared to listen and wants to know how others perceive his behavior.

In asking for feedback, however, it is important to follow some of the same guidelines as for giving feedback. For example, a person should be specific about the subject on which he wants feedback. The individual who says to the group,

"I would like the group to tell me what they think about me" may receive more feedback than he planned. In addition, the request is so general that the group members may be uncertain about where to begin or which behaviors are relevant to the request. In these cases, other group members can help the receiver by asking such questions as "Can you be more specific?" or "About what do you want feedback?" Feedback is a reciprocal process; both senders and receivers can help each other in soliciting and in giving it. Sometimes it is also important to provide feedback on how a person is giving feedback. If a receiver is upset, hurt, or angry, other group members can say to the sender, "Look how you told him that; I would be angry, too" or "What other way could you have given him the same information without evaluating him or degrading him?" It is desirable to give feedback so that the receiver can preserve his self-esteem.

Many people want to know how their behavior is being perceived by others, but they fear the consequences of asking for such information. How easily a person will ask for feedback is related to the amount of trust in the interpersonal relationship. However, people fear that the receiver will use their feedback (particularly negative feedback) to reinforce his negative feelings about himself. Again, it is sometimes difficult for a person to separate his behavior from his feelings of self-worth.

Unmodifiable vs. Modifiable Behavior

To be effective, feedback should be aimed at behavior that is relatively easy to change. Many individuals' behaviors are habitual and could be described as a personal style developed through years of behaving and responding in certain ways. Feedback on this kind of behavior often is frustrating because the behavior can be very difficult to change.

Feedback on behaviors that are difficult to change may often make the person self-conscious and anxious about his behavior. For example, if the wife of a chain smoker gives him feedback (using all of the appropriate guidelines) about his smoking behavior, it would still be very difficult for him to change. Chain-smoking is a behavior determined by often-unknown causes. The individual may smoke to reduce his tension level; continuous feedback on his smoking behavior may only increase his tension. Consequently, he smokes more to reduce that tension.

Occasionally, in giving feedback, one must determine whether the behavior represents an individual's life style or results from some unknown personality factors. Sometimes it may be helpful first to ask the receiver whether he perceives his behavior as modifiable. Many behaviors can be easily changed through feedback and the person's conscious desire to change his behavior in order to produce a more effective interpersonal style.

Motivation to Hurt vs. Motivation to Help

It is assumed that the primary motivation of membership in growth groups is to help oneself and others to grow. When an individual is angry, however, his motivation may be to hurt the other person. Frequently, the conflict turns into win-lose strategies in which the goal of the interaction is to degrade the other person. It is difficult when one is angry to consider that the needs of the other person are as important as one's own. Angry feedback may be useless, even when the information is potentially helpful, because the receiver may need to reject the feedback in order to protect his integrity.

Coping with Anger

There are several ways to cope with anger. One is to engage in a verbal or physical attack that frequently increases in intensity. Another method to deal with anger is to suppress it. One consequence of this strategy, however, is that the individual builds internal pressure to the point that he can lose control of his behavior. A third—

and better—method is to talk about personal feelings of anger without assigning responsibility for them to the other person. Focusing on personal feelings may frequently encourage other group members to help the individual. In this way the anger dissipates without either viciousness or suppression. Anger and conflict are not themselves "bad." Angry feelings are as legitimate as any other feelings. Conflict can be a growth-producing phenomenon. It is the manner in which conflict or angry feelings are handled that can have negative consequences. Only through surfacing and resolving conflicts can people develop competence and confidence in dealing with these feelings and situations. Part of the benefit derived from growth groups is learning to express anger or to resolve conflicts in constructive, problem-solving ways.

CONCLUSION

The process of giving feedback obviously would be hampered if one attempted to consider *all* of the above guidelines. Some are needed more frequently than others: i.e., feedback should be descriptive, nonevaluative, specific, and should embody freedom of choice. These guidelines can also be used diagnostically. For example, when the person receiving feedback reacts defensively, some of the guidelines have probably been violated. Group members can ask the receiver how he heard the feedback and help the giver assess how he gave it.

Giving feedback effectively may depend on an individual's values and basic philosophy about himself, about his relationships with others, and about other people in general. Certain guidelines, however, can be learned and are valuable in helping people give and receive effective and useful feedback.

Appendix C
POSTMEETING REACTIONS FORM

Directions: You are to rank-order each statement in each set from 1 (most like) to 10 (least like) to describe the meeting and your behavior. Use this procedure: In each set, first identify the statement you would rank 1, then the one you would rank 10, then 2, then 9—alternating toward the middle of the scale.

The meeting was like this:

(   ) There was much warmth and friendliness.

(   ) There was much aggressive behavior.

(   ) People were uninterested and uninvolved.

(   ) People tried to dominate and take over.

(   ) We were in need of help.

(   ) Much of the conversation was irrelevant.

(   ) We were strictly task-oriented.

(   ) The members were very polite.

(   ) There was much underlying irritation.

(   ) We worked on our process issues.

My behavior was like this:

(   ) I was warm and friendly to some.

(   ) I did not participate much.

(   ) I concentrated on the job.

(   ) I tried to get everyone involved.

(   ) I took over the leadership.

(   ) I was polite to all.

(   ) My suggestions were frequently off the point.

(   ) I was a follower.

(   ) I was irritated.

(   ) I was eager and aggressive.

Reprinted from J. William Pfeiffer and John E. Jones (Eds.), *A Handbook of Structured Experiences for Human Relations Training* (Vol. III, Rev.), La Jolla, Calif.: University Associates, 1974. Used with permission of the publisher.

Appendix D
GROUP-GROWTH EVALUATION FORM

Directions: Rate your group on each characteristic as the group was initially and as it is now. Use a seven-point scale with 7 as the highest rating.

Climate

Initially   Now

_____   _____   1. I am treated as a human being, not as just another group member.

_____   _____   2. I feel close to the members of this group.

_____   _____   3. This group displays cooperation and teamwork.

_____   _____   4. Membership in this group is aiding my personal growth.

_____   _____   5. I have trust and confidence in the other members of this group.

_____   _____   6. Members of this group show supportive behavior toward each other.

_____   _____   7. I derive satisfaction from my membership in this group.

_____   _____   8. I feel psychologically close to this group.

_____   _____   9. I get a sense of accomplishment from my membership in this group.

_____   10. I am being honest in responding to this evaluation.

Data Flow

Initially   Now

_____   _____   11. I am willing to share information with other members of the group.

_____   _____   12. I feel free to discuss important personal matters with group members.

Reprinted from J. William Pfeiffer and John E. Jones (Eds.), *A Handbook of Structured Experiences for Human Relations Training* (Vol. III, Rev.), La Jolla, Calif.: University Associates, 1974. Used with permission of the publisher.

Goal Formation

Initially **Now**

———— ———— 13. I am oriented toward personal goals rather than toward group objectives.

———— ———— 14. This group uses integrative, constructive methods in problem-solving, rather than a competitive approach.

———— ———— 15. I am able to deal promptly and well with the important problems of this group.

———— ———— 16. The activities of this group reflect a constructive integration of the needs and desires of its members.

———— ———— 17. My needs and desires are reflected in the activities of this group.

Control

Initially **Now**

———— ———— 18. This group has a real sense of responsibility for getting a job done.

———— ———— 19. I feel manipulated by the group.

———— ———— 20. I think that I manipulate the group.

Appendix G
PROCESS OBSERVER RECORDING FORM

Record verbal and non verbal behaviors engaged in by specific members of the group in the section on this form assigned to you. Guide your observations by the statements and questions included in your section. Try to focus on the *processes* that emerge in the meeting rather than on the *content* of what is said. Imagine that you are a process consultant called in by this group to assist it in improving its internal functioning.

I. *Structure:* how the group organizes to accomplish its task. What ground rules emerge? What leadership behaviors are displayed? How are decisions made? How is information treated?

II. *Climate:* the psychological atmosphere of the meeting. How are feelings (as opposed to points of view) dealt with. What nonverbal behavior indicates changes in climate? How do members' voices denote feeling tone?

III. *Facilitation:* how group members influence the development of the group. Does the group process itself? What group-building behaviors (bringing in silent members, harmonizing conflict, reinforcing participation, etc.) are engaged in?

IV. *Dysfunctions:* behaviors that hinder the accomplishment of the group's task. What anti-group behaviors (blocking, recognition-seeking, dominating, withdrawing, etc.) are seen? What communication patterns develop that are dysfunctional to the group?

V. *Convergence:* how the group moves from independence to collective judgement. What behaviors promote agreement? What consensus-seeking behaviors are observed? What "false" consensus behaviors (such as "me too," "I'll go along with that,") are displayed?

Reprinted from John E. Jones and J. William Pfeiffer (Eds.), *The 1973 Annual Handbook for Group Facilitators*, La Jolla, Calif.: University Associates, 1973. Used with permission of the publisher.

Appendix H
MEETING APPRAISAL FORM

Directions: Please give your candid reactions to this meeting by rating it on the seven-point scale shown below. Circle the appropriate number on the scale to represent your evaluation. Your comments are appreciated.

1. What did you think of the meeting?

<table>
<tr><td>A waste
of time</td><td>1   2   3   4   5   6   7
_____</td><td>Much was
accomplished</td></tr>
</table>

2. What should have been done to improve the meeting? List suggestions.

3. What should the leader have done? List suggestions.

4. What might you have done to help the meeting?

AAO 7162